Jossey-Bass Teacher

Jossey-Bass Teacher provides educators with practical knowledge and tools to create a positive and lifelong impact on student learning. We offer classroom-tested and research-based teaching resources for a variety of grade levels and subject areas. Whether you are an aspiring, new, or veteran teacher, we want to help you make every teaching day your best.

From ready-to-use classroom activities to the latest teaching framework, our value-packed books provide insightful, practical, and comprehensive materials on the topics that matter most to K–12 teachers. We hope to become your trusted source for the best ideas from the most experienced and respected experts in the field.

i-SAFE Internet Safety Activities

Reproducible Projects for Teachers and Parents, Grades K–8

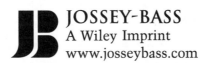

JOSSEY-BASS
A Wiley Imprint
www.josseybass.com

Published by Jossey-Bass
A Wiley Imprint
989 Market Street, San Francisco, CA 94103-1741—www.josseybass.com

Jossey-Bass books and products are available through most bookstores. To contact Jossey-Bass directly call our Customer Care Department within the U.S. at 800-956-7739, outside the U.S. at 317-572-3986, or fax 317-572-4002.

Jossey-Bass also publishes its books in a variety of electronic formats. Some content that appears in print may not be available in electronic books.

ISBN: 978-0-470-53952-1

Printed in the United States of America.
FIRST EDITION

PB Printing 10 9 8 7 6 5 4 3 2 1

About the Book

i-SAFE Internet Safety Activities: Reproducible Projects for Teachers and Parents is a resource for teaching Internet safety for parents, teachers, and those in other educational environments, such as clubs or after-school programs. The activities allow students to learn about Internet safety in an engaging, self-directed manner and are designed to challenge students to develop critical-thinking skills. Students who do the projects will be empowered to age-appropriately share Internet safety awareness and knowledge with their peers, their parents, and their communities.

In the lower grades, activity pages are designed to reinforce concepts introduced by the instructor. In upper-grade levels, sections can be completed by the student in a self-guided manner. Each level includes group interaction and empowerment activities to promote and support best practices in effective Internet safety and responsible use of the Internet in education.

Teacher's Guide sections in each chapter provide discussion guidance, answers to activity questions, and, where applicable, tips for reinforcing school "acceptable use policies" (AUP) with the activity concepts. Students are also encouraged to complete an assessment survey, online and anonymously, before beginning the first lesson (pre-assessments), after their final activity (post-assessments), and three to six weeks after completion (outcomes assessments). A key component of the i-SAFE program is a focus on students' Internet behaviors and dispositions (beliefs, interests, personal feelings) toward the Internet. As the i-SAFE curriculum continues to evolve, several different forms of curriculum-based assessments, student learning, and Internet behaviors and dispositions have also evolved. i-SAFE's assessments are grounded in new conceptions of students' Internet safety behavior changes and dispositions; they are generic across grade levels and are designed to be electronically accessed and processed. The information i-SAFE collects from the program participants is important to help us understand the impact of the total program. The assessments for students target three core questions: (1) What do students report about their Internet behaviors and dispositions before they participate in the i-SAFE program (pre-assessments)? (2) What do students learn as a result of the completion of the i-SAFE lessons (post-assessments)? and (3) To what extent have students changed their Internet behaviors and dispositions as a result of their i-SAFE learning experience? The knowledge that students gain as a result of their learning in the i-SAFE core curriculum is important. However, i-SAFE believes that actual changes in students' use of the Internet and in their disposition toward the Internet, that align with being safe on the Internet, are closer to the long-range goals of the total i-SAFE effort.

Table A.1 provides the scope of the chapters in the book and alignment to National Technology Standards, which are presented in Table A.2.

Table A.1

Chapter	Chapter Goal	Standards Alignment
1. Diving into Internet Safety (Grades K–1)	The overall goals of the lesson are to (a) provide exposure to vocabulary words related to the Internet and (b) gain a basic awareness of a comparison of the physical community to the abstract concept of Cyberspace as a community. Throughout the lesson/activities, learners age-appropriately begin to develop an understanding of the need to make responsible online choices, beginning with always having an adult's help when going online to ensure personal safety.	National Educational Technology Standards for Students (NETS-S): The Next Generation Standards 1, 2, 4, and 5
2. Online Safari (Grades 2–4)	The overall goals of the lesson are to (a) provide exposure to vocabulary words related to the Internet and (b) gain a basic awareness of a comparison of the physical community to the abstract concept of Cyberspace as a community. Throughout the lesson/activities, learners age-appropriately begin to develop an understanding of the need to make responsible online choices, beginning with always having an adult's help when going online to ensure personal safety.	National Educational Technology Standards for Students (NETS-S): The Next Generation Standards 1, 2, 4, and 5
3. Heroes Against Cyber Bullying (Grades 3–4)	The overall goals of the lesson are to (a) provide exposure to vocabulary related to cyber bullying and netiquette and (b) gain an awareness of safety in online interactions. Throughout the lesson/activities, learners will develop an understanding of the concept of "netiquette" and how it applies to online behaviors and interactions.	National Educational Technology Standards for Students (NETS-S): The Next Generation Standards 1, 2, 4, and 5
4. Managing Personal Information Online (Grades 5–8)	The overall goals of the lesson are to (a) provide exposure to vocabulary words related to the Internet and (b) gain a basic awareness of the types of information students reveal when online and how to stay safer. Throughout the lesson/activities, learners are asked to consider what they reveal through screen names, passwords, profiles, and more and to carefully consider what they are doing before acting.	National Educational Technology Standards for Students (NETS-S): The Next Generation Standards 1, 2, 4, 5, and 6

5. A Common-Sense Approach to Strangers Online (Grades 5–8)	The overall goals of the lesson are to (a) provide exposure to vocabulary related to online safety and strangers and (b) gain an awareness of safety in online interactions. Throughout the lesson/activities, learners will develop an understanding of the need to make responsible choices to ensure personal safety.	National Educational Technology Standards for Students (NETS-S): The Next Generation Standards 1, 2, 4, 5, and 6
6. Cyber Bullying Prevention: Citizenship and Netiquette Sense (Grades 5–8)	The overall goals of the lesson are to (a) provide exposure to vocabulary related to cyber bullying and netiquette and (b) gain an awareness of safety in online interactions. Throughout the lesson/activities, learners will develop an understanding of the concept of "netiquette" and how it applies to online behaviors and interactions.	National Educational Technology Standards for Students (NETS-S): The Next Generation Standards 1, 2, 4, 5, and 6

Table A.2. National Educational Technology Standards for Students

I. Creativity and Innovation
Students demonstrate creative thinking, construct knowledge, and develop innovative products and processes using technology. Students: A. Apply existing knowledge to generate new ideas, products, or processes. B. Create original works as a means of personal or group expression. C. Use models and simulations to explore complex systems and issues. D. Identify trends and forecast possibilities.

II. Communication and Collaboration
Students use digital media and environments to communicate and work collaboratively, including at a distance, to support individual learning and contribute to the learning of others. Students: A. Interact, collaborate, and publish with peers, experts, or others employing a variety of digital environments and media. B. Communicate information and ideas effectively to multiple audiences using a variety of media and formats. C. Develop cultural understanding and global awareness by engaging with learners of other cultures. D. Contribute to project teams to produce original works or solve problems.

IV. Critical Thinking, Problem Solving, and Decision Making
Students use critical thinking skills to plan and conduct research, manage projects, solve problems, and make informed decisions using appropriate digital tools and resources. Students: A. Identify and define authentic problems and significant questions for investigation. B. Plan and manage activities to develop a solution or complete a project. C. Collect and analyze data to identify solutions and/or make informed decisions. D. Use multiple processes and diverse perspectives to explore alternative solutions.

V. Digital Citizenship

Students understand human, cultural, and societal issues related to technology and practice legal and ethical behavior. Students:

A. Advocate and practice safe, legal, and responsible use of information and technology.

B. Exhibit a positive attitude toward using technology that supports collaboration, learning, and productivity.

C. Demonstrate personal responsibility for lifelong learning.

D. Exhibit leadership for digital citizenship.

VI. Technology Operations and Concepts

Students demonstrate a sound understanding of technology concepts, systems, and operations. Students:

A. Understand and use technology systems.

B. Select and use applications effectively and productively.

C. Troubleshoot systems and applications.

D. Transfer current knowledge to learning of new technologies.

About the Author

Founded in 1998 and active in all fifty states, i-SAFE Inc. (**www.isafe.org**) is the leader in e-Safety education. i-SAFE is a nonprofit corporation whose mission is to educate and empower students to safely and responsibly take control of their Internet experiences. i-SAFE provides knowledge that enables them to recognize and avoid dangerous, destructive, or unlawful online behavior and to respond appropriately. This is accomplished through dynamic K through 12 curriculum and community-outreach programs. i-SAFE is the only comprehensive e-Safety program available that incorporates community outreach and youth empowerment in education-based materials.

i-SAFE's education component provides students with up-to-date, interactive, and age-appropriate e-Safety curriculum lessons covering a full spectrum of topics ranging from cyber bullying prevention and response to safety on social networking sites and the legal use of intellectual property found online. The prevention-oriented curriculum employs peer-to-peer communication and cooperative learning activities to help students retain this valuable information. The outreach component facilitates the extension of students' newly acquired e-Safety knowledge beyond the classrooms and effectively raises awareness about online safety throughout the community. Youth empowerment is the link. Students are encouraged to become student mentors who communicate i-SAFE's online safety message via peer-to-peer contact and exciting community-wide activities, events, and rallies. Since 2002, more than twenty-eight million students have been educated and empowered through i-SAFE's education and outreach programs to be safe and responsible online citizens.

At the same time, i-SAFE's professional development training prepares educators to teach the i-SAFE curriculum. Similar i-SAFE trainings for parents, for adults over the age of fifty, and for law enforcement educate and raise awareness about Internet safety in communities across the country.

Contents

Unit 1: Diving into Internet Safety (K–1)

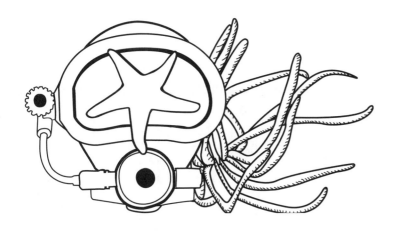

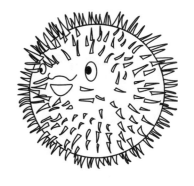

Unit 1: Diving into Internet Safety (K-1) Teacher's Guide

 ## Unit Goal

Throughout the lesson/activities, learners will begin to develop an understanding of the need to make responsible choices, beginning with always having an adult's help when going on-line to ensure personal safety. Students will engage in a group discussion moderated by the teacher to (a) provide exposure to vocabulary words related to the Internet, and (b) gain a basic awareness of a comparison of the physical community to the abstract concept of Cyberspace as a community.

 ## Understanding the Unit Format

This guide will provide you with discussion guidance, answers to activity questions, and explanations of the content of the student pages. Where applicable, this guide will also provide tips for reinforcing your acceptable use policies (AUP) with the activity concepts.

Diving Into Internet Safety lesson/activity sections include:

1.1.   Diving Into Internet Safety

1.2.   Ways to Learn

1.3.   It's About Internet Safety!

1.4.   Fish Swim Together!

1.5.   A School Is a Community Too

1.6.   Undersea Maze

1.7.   Exploring Safely Online

1.8.   Vocabulary and Concept Review

1.9.   Tell About Internet Safety

1.10.   i-SAFE Assessment

Additional Resources

Refer to the i-SAFE *i-EDUCATOR Times* newsletters located at www.isafe.org and general i-SAFE lesson plans on similar topics for additional resource materials and background information if needed.

Prepare for the Lesson

Pre-Assessment

- If beginning the i-SAFE program with this unit, administer the pre-assessment online at http://www.isafe.org/activitybook.
- Enter School ID# 24615.

Post-Assessment

- If you will end the i-SAFE program with this unit, have students complete the post-assessment online at http://www.isafe.org/activitybook.
- Students complete the Outcomes assessment three to six weeks after completion of the last i-SAFE lesson implemented.

Plan Your Format

This unit is designed to enable transition from traditional class lessons to a more self-guided format, depending on student reading abilities.

1. Arrange for students to take the online pre-assessment.
2. Review the student activity pages and determine how you will implement the unit.
3. *Optional:* Prepare any additional reference material of your choice, including Internet access.
4. Provide each student with a copy of the student pages and review directions for student use.

Implementation Options

The following are suggested options for implementing the unit.

Group guided: Use the activities as short lessons over a period of time (one or two weeks to complete). This option is especially recommended for students with less developed reading comprehension skills.

- Have students complete the online pre-assessment prior to engaging in the i-SAFE program.
- Assign and go over each activity page with the class as a large group and have students complete them as instructed. You may want to have students read over text parts together to reinforce meaning.
- Go over completed pages with the group as they are finished.
- Have students complete the online post-assessment.
- Complete the empowerment activity suggested, or create your own activity.

Small groups: Students work in groups to complete the activities. This may be done in several sessions.

- Have students complete the online pre-assessment prior to engaging in the i-SAFE program.
- Introduce the unit with the pre-activity discussion.
- Create small work groups of three to four students.
- Student groups complete the assigned pages for each session and discuss their answers within the group.
- Go over the Wrap-Up activity to review the concepts presented in the unit.
- Have students complete the online post-assessment.
- Complete the empowerment activity suggested, or create your own activity.

Semi-self-guided: This option should only be considered for age-proficient readers. Create a timeline for activities to be completed.

- Have students complete the online pre-assessment prior to engaging in the i-SAFE program.
- Introduce the unit with the Activity 1 discussion.
- Have students complete their assignments.
- Go over the Wrap-Up activity to review the concepts.
- Have students complete the online post-assessment.
- Complete the empowerment activity suggested, or create your own activity.

Doing the Activities

1.1. Diving into Internet Safety (page 12)

Introduce i-Buddy with the finger puppet activity.

 Materials Needed

- Crayons or markers
- Scissors
- Tape

Discuss

Introduce i-Buddy as a character who wants to help us with activities to learn about Internet safety. Provide open-ended prompts and questions to engage students in discussion. Include the following:

- Ask students to define the word "Internet" (answers will vary).
- How do we get to the Internet? (Use a computer.)

- How many have been on the Internet, or have watched someone while he or she was on the Internet?"
- For those who are familiar with the Internet, ask who helps them go on the Internet.
- Ask students to brainstorm about what they think "learning about Internet safety" means.

Discuss answers. Lead students to define it as knowing how to be safe when using computers to get on the Internet. Explain that it also means learning how to use computers the right way.

Note: For those who have not yet been on the Internet, explain that even if they haven't been on the Internet yet, they will be soon and therefore need to learn about it.

i-Buddy's Message

Inform the children that i-Buddy has a special message for each one of them to remember. The message is: You will make the Internet safe if you get help from an adult. Then it will be fun for everybody.

Optional Online Extension Activity

If you have Internet access in the classroom, log on to the Internet at this time, and visit www.isafe.org. Click on the "i-MENTOR Training Network" link under "Kids and Teens." Have the students find i-Buddy. Return to the "Kids and Teens" page or http://xblock.isafe.org and explore with your students to demonstrate an example of using the Internet.

Making the Finger Puppet

Have the students turn to the activity page. Have them color the picture and cut it out on the dotted lines. Tape the tabs together to make a finger puppet.

Option:

1. Cut out the shape of i-Buddy from felt, and glue on the features.
2. Enlarge and cut out to make an armband.

Hidden Picture Activity

Students circle the hidden objects. When finished, have students name the items they found that have to do with computers.

1.2. Ways to Learn (page 14)

Students will complete these activities to introduce and/or review information about what people do on the Internet and to reinforce the opportunities to learn online.

- Ask students whether they know what the phrase "going online" means.

- Have students name things they can do on the Internet. Reinforce that the Internet is used to have fun and to learn.
- Have students go over the Internet places shown/listed on page 15.

Optional Online Extension Activity

Use your school Web site as an example of an Internet site.

1.3. It's About Internet Safety! (page 16)

Introduce the concept of Internet safety.

As a class, define "Internet safety" by providing open-ended prompts and questions to prompt discussion. Include the following and provide time for student responses after each prompt:

- What is Internet safety? (Things we can learn and do to keep ourselves and our computers safe when using the Internet.)
- Have students identify things they can do to keep a computer from getting broken. (Answers will vary depending on age of learners.)
- Introduce concept: one thing everyone who goes on the Internet needs to know is that sometimes going online can be unsafe for people.
- *Review:* Who can remember i-Buddy's special message? (You will make the Internet safe if you get help from an adult. Then it will be fun for everybody.)
- *Introduce a concept:* Another way to stay safe on the Internet is to work with a friend or other trusted adult (older sibling, teacher, etc.). If you don't understand something, you will have help.
- Have students complete the dot-to-dot i-Buddy and Circle of Friends activities.

1.4. Fish Swim Together! (page 18)

Make a simple comparison of the physical community to the cyber community by providing open-ended prompts and questions to promote discussion. Include the following and provide time for student responses after each prompt:

- What is a community? (The area where we live, which contains places where we know real people.)
- Have students identify places they like to go to in the community.
- What does the word "Cyberspace" mean? (A community, which contains places to visit, just like in the real community, is called the cyber community.)
- Do you know that the Internet is a community a lot like the one we live in?

We say the Internet is a community because it has the same kinds of places in it that we have in the communities we live in, and real people go to those places.

Explain that schools of fish are also an example of a community in that they swim together. The fish need each other to stay safe. They let each other know when they see danger.

Have students complete the activity page. **Instructions:** On the top half of the page: number each fish in the school of fish and color them.

Use the activity page to reinforce the concept that friends help keep each other safe while on the Internet by helping each other to follow the rules when using a computer and the Internet.

1.5. A School Is a Community Too (page 19)

- **Review:** When people go into Cyberspace, they need to depend on people they know to help keep them safe.
- The main way for children to stay safe on the Internet is to ask for the help of an adult.
- At school when you need help or have a question, who do you ask?
- **Question:** Who do you ask for help at home?

Have students complete the activity page. **Instructions:** In the space draw a picture of an adult who helps you on the computer. Fill in the blank in the sentence at the bottom of the page: _____ helps me on the computer at school.

> **AUP Tip:** Use this activity as reinforcement for your school's acceptable use policy (AUP) by reinforcing who will help students at school when they use computers and/or go on the Internet.

1.6. Undersea Maze (page 20)

Present the idea: "For you, most of the rules you follow are made by your parents and your teachers. Parents protect their children by making rules for them to follow when they are out in the community."

Question: "What are some of the rules that your parents have made?" Provide time for students to respond. (Answers should include don't talk to strangers, tell your parents where you are going, wear your seatbelt, look both ways when you cross the street, stop for a red light, etc.)

Question: "If we don't follow rules what could happen?"

Question: "Why do parents think their children need rules?" (To keep them safe.)

Review: We have learned that:

- Rules are made to keep people safe.
- Parents keep their children safe by making rules for them to follow when they are out in the community.

- When you follow the rules of your community, you are a good citizen.
- When you follow the rules in the cyber community, you are a good cyber citizen.

Apply It!

- Have students give examples of safety rules to follow when swimming or going in the water.
- Have students complete the Undersea Maze. *Instructions:* Help i-Buddy swim to safety. List two things you do that keep you safe in the water.

1.7. Exploring Safely Online (page 21)

AUP Tip: Use this activity as reinforcement for your school's acceptable use policy (AUP) by reinforcing class and school policies on how to use technology equipment responsibly.

Use the Internet safety tips on this page to reinforce the need for adult assistance and/or permission before accessing the Internet.

Internet Safety Tips

1. Get permission from an adult before you go on the Internet.
2. Tell a trusted adult right away if you read or see anything online that makes you feel uncomfortable.

Depending on age level, discuss what it means to feel uncomfortable and to see something that makes one feel uncomfortable.

Apply It!

Have students list or draw a picture of two rules that they will follow to stay safe on the Internet. Have students share the rules they came up with.

1.8. Vocabulary and Concept Review (page 22)

Have students complete the word practice and word jumble activities as appropriate to their age and developmental levels.

1.9. Tell About Internet Safety (page 24)
Apply It!

Students will:

- Write and/or draw a picture of a good rule to follow when using the Internet.
- Cut out around the fish shape.

Assist students in creating poster(s) or a bulletin board to share what they have learned with others.

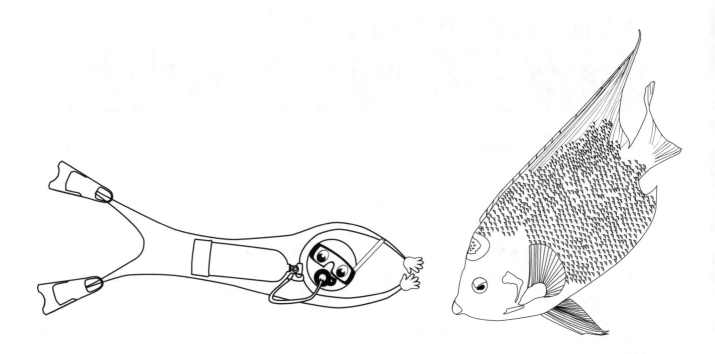

1.10. Assessment Page

Have each student complete the Student Assessments page (four questions).

Read each item out loud, and provide time for the students to circle their answers before going on to the next item. Reinforce that it is okay if they do not understand a question or are not sure of an answer.

Question 1: Have the students look for the picture of the house next to the number 1. Read the question and instruct the students to circle "YES" if they use a computer at home or "NO" if they do not have or do not use a computer at home.

Question 2: Have the students look for the number 2 in the box with the pictures of the girl using a computer. Read the question and instruct the students to circle "YES" if they go on the Internet, "NO" if they do not go on the Internet, or "I DON'T KNOW" if they are not sure or do not understand the question.

Question 3: Have the students look for the picture of the e-mail (just like i-Buddy's e-mail from the lesson) next to the number 3. Instruct the students to circle "YES" if they use e-mail, "NO" if they don't use e-mail yet, or "I DON'T KNOW" if they are not sure or do not understand the question.

Question 4: Have the students look for the picture of the boy and girl using computers next to the number 4. Instruct the students to circle "YES" if they chat on the Internet, "NO" if they don't chat, or "I DON'T KNOW" if they are not sure, or do not understand the question.

When students have finished, collect the pages.

Ask the students how many have shared what they have learned about Internet safety with their parents. You will need this information for the online assessment form.

Complete the Online Assessment Form

Your participation in the assessment process is of vital importance in underscoring the need for Internet safety education, assessing the effectiveness of the program, developing future needs, and providing validation to our funding organizations.

- Complete the Online Assessment form after completion of i-SAFE program, based on the answers provided by the students and your experience implementing the curriculum.
- **Do Not Send Student Assessment Pages to i-SAFE.**
- Access the Online Assessments at http://www.isafe.org/activitybook.

Note: Use one online form for every one hundred students or fewer. If you are responding for more than one hundred students, please complete more than one online form as necessary.

1.1. Diving into Internet Safety

 ## Learn About It

i-Buddy is here to help you learn about using computers and the Internet safely.

 ## Activity
i-Buddy Finger Puppet

Cut around the i-Buddy figure, and tape the tabs together to make a finger puppet.

Options

1. Cut out the shape of i-Buddy and glue on the features.
2. Enlarge and cut out to make an armband.

Color me!   **Cut me!**

Activity
Hidden Picture

Instructions: Select an item from the group on the right and then circle where it is hidden in the picture on the left.

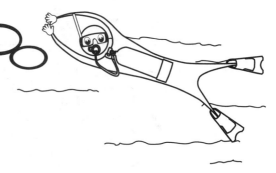

You will make the Internet safe if you get help from an adult. Then it will be fun for everyone.

1.2. Ways to Learn

 Learn About It

i-Buddy likes to learn about fish and the ocean.
Circle the one in each row that is different.

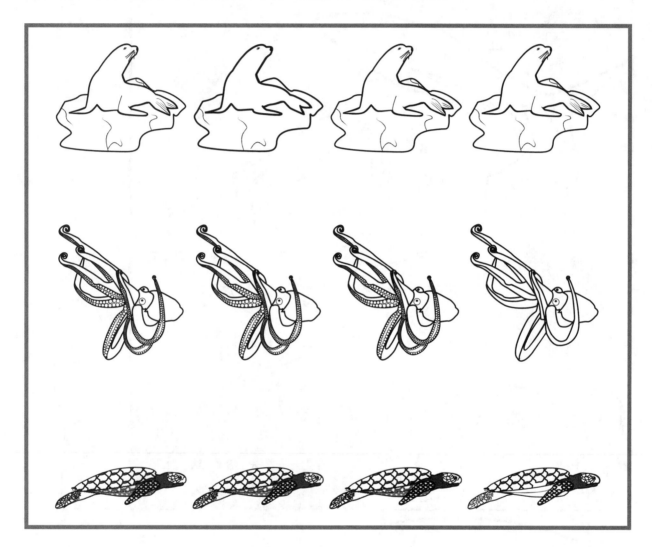

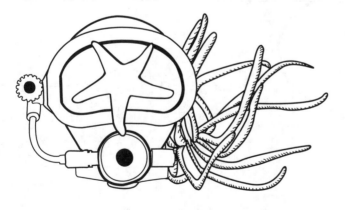 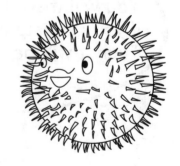

There's another way to learn about the ocean—or about anything!

We can use a computer to get on the Internet.

We call it going online!

People use the Internet to do lots of things.

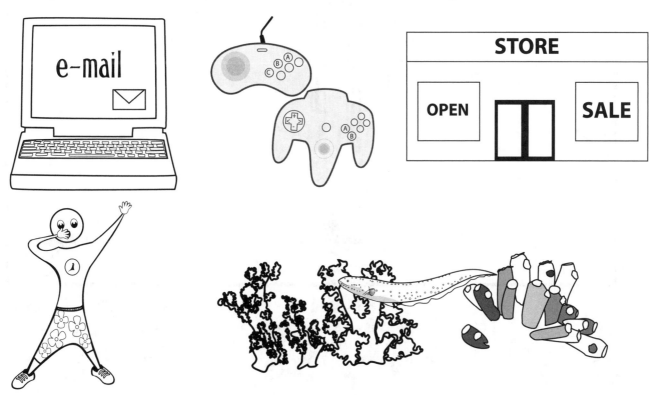

1.3. It's About Internet Safety

 Learn About It

 Activity
dot-to-dot i-Buddy

You will make the Internet safe if you get help from an adult. Then it will be fun for everyone.

Circle of Friends

Instructions: Draw yourself in the middle.

WE CAN HELP EACH OTHER TO STAY SAFE ONLINE

1.4. Fish Swim Together!

 ## Activity
Fish Swim Together!

Instructions: Number each fish in the school and color it.

1.5. A School Is a Community Too

Activity

A School Is a Community Too

Instructions: In the space below, draw a picture of an adult who helps you on the computer.

Communities depend on each other for help.

Finish the Sentence:

_____ helps me on the computer at school.

1.6. Undersea Maze

 ## Activity
Undersea Maze

Instructions: Help i-Buddy swim to safety.

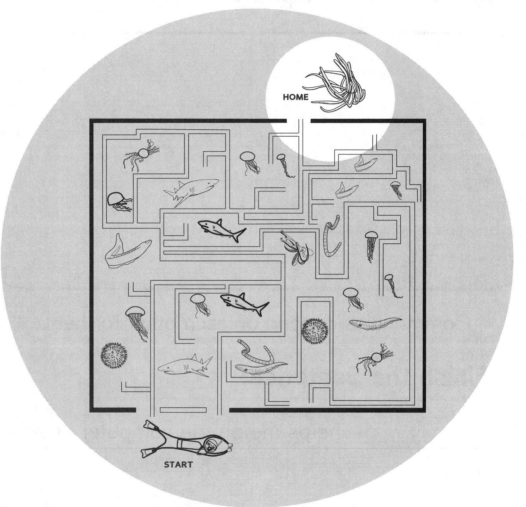

 ## Apply It

List two things you do that keep you safe in the water.

_____

_____

_____

An adult helps you stay safe in the water.

1.7. Exploring Safely Online

Internet Safety Tips

1. Get permission from an adult before you go on the Internet.
2. Tell a trusted adult right away if you read or see anything online that makes you feel uncomfortable.

 Apply It!

List or draw a picture of two rules that you will follow to stay safe on the Internet.

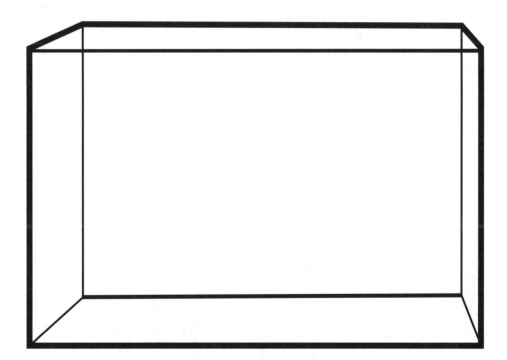

An adult helps you stay safe on the Internet.

I.8. Vocabulary and Concept Review

 Apply It
Word Practice

Instructions: Copy the words below.

Cyberspace _____

Internet _____

i-Buddy _____

Computer _____

Adult _____

Instructions: Trace the sentence.

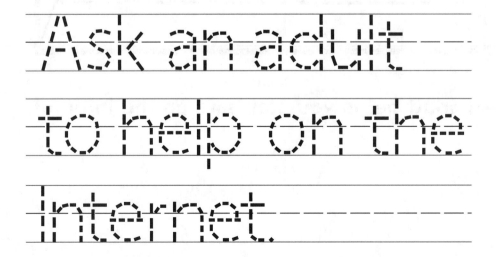

Ask an adult
to help on the
Internet.

Apply It
Word Jumbles

Instructions: Arrange the words in each list to make a sentence. Write each new sentence.

Level 1

Internet, safe, on, be, the

_____

_____

_____

_____

Level 2

in, helps, us, Cyberspace, i-Buddy

_____

_____

_____

_____

Level 3

of, is, Cyberspace, real, a, community, people

_____

_____

_____

_____

1.9. Tell About Internet Safety

Apply It

Diving into Internet Safety

Instructions: Write and/or draw a picture of a good rule to follow when using the Internet. Cut out around the fish shape to add to a poster or bulletin board.

1.10. Student Assessment

Do you use a computer at home?

Yes   No   I don't know

Do you go on the Internet?

Yes   No   I don't know

Do you use e-mail?

Yes   No   I don't know

Do you chat on the Internet?

Yes   No   I don't know

Unit 2: Online Safari (2–4)

 ## Unit Goal

Throughout the lesson/activities, learners will begin to develop an understanding of the need to make responsible choices, beginning with always having an adult's help when going online, to ensure personal safety. Students will engage in a group discussion moderated by the teacher to (a) provide exposure to vocabulary words related to the Internet and (b) gain a basic awareness of a comparison of the physical community to the abstract concept of Cyberspace as a community.

 ## Understanding the Unit Format

This guide will provide you with discussion guidance, answers to activity questions, and explanations of the content of the student pages. Where applicable, this guide will also provide tips for reinforcing your acceptable use policies (AUP) with the activity concepts.

Online Safari lesson/activity sections include:

2.1.   Going on Safari

2.2.   Safety in the Community

2.3.   Jungle Sights and Online Sites

2.4.   Safety Tips

2.5.   E-mail Safety

2.6.   Safari Health Check

2.7.   Learn About Attachments

2.8.   Community Crossword Puzzle

2.9.   Apply What You Have Learned Mini-Book

Additional Resources

Refer to the i-SAFE *i-EDUCATOR Times* newsletters located at http://www.isafe.org and general i-SAFE lesson plans on similar topics for additional resource materials and background information if needed.

Prepare for the Lesson
Pre-Assessment

- If beginning the i-SAFE program with this unit, administer the pre-assessment online at http://www.isafe.org/activitybook.
- Enter School ID# 24615.

Post-Assessment

- If you will end the i-SAFE program with this unit, have students complete the post-assessment online at http://www.isafe.org/activitybook.
- Students complete the Outcomes assessment three to six weeks after completion of the last i-SAFE lesson implemented.

Plan Your Format

This unit is designed to enable transition from traditional class lessons to a more self-guided format, depending on student reading abilities.

1. Arrange for students to take the online pre-assessment.
2. Review the student activity pages and determine how you will implement the unit.
3. *Optional:* Prepare any additional reference material of your choice, including Internet access.
4. Provide each student with a copy of the student pages and review directions for student use.

Implementation Options

The following are suggested options for implementing the unit.

Group guided: Use the activities as short lessons over a period of time (one or two weeks to complete). This option is especially recommended for students with less developed reading comprehension skills.

- Have students complete the online pre-assessment prior to engaging in the i-SAFE program.
- Assign and go over each activity page with the class as a large group and have students complete them as instructed. You may want to have students read over text parts together to reinforce meaning.
- Go over completed pages with the group as they are finished.
- Have students complete the online post-assessment.
- Complete the empowerment activity suggested, or create your own activity.

Small groups: Students work in groups to complete the activities. This may be done in several sessions.

- Have students complete the online pre-assessment prior to engaging in the i-SAFE program.
- Introduce the unit with the Activity 1 discussion.
- Create small work groups of three to four students.
- Student groups complete the assigned pages for each session and discuss their answers within the group.
- Go over the Wrap-Up activity to review the concepts presented in the unit.
- Have students complete the online post-assessment.
- Complete the empowerment activity suggested, or create your own activity.

Semi-self-guided: Create a timeline for sections of the unit to be completed.

- Have students complete the online pre-assessment prior to engaging in the i-SAFE program.
- Introduce the unit with the Activity 1 discussion.
- Students complete their assignments.
- Go over the Wrap-Up activity to review the concepts.
- Have students complete the online post-assessment.
- Complete the empowerment activity suggested, or create your own activity.

Doing the Activities

2.1. Going on Safari (page 37)

Go over the introduction at the top of the first page to introduce the unit:

Explain that traveling in the online community can be a lot like going on safari. You can explore places you've never been before, but you need to be careful too. You need to be aware of your surroundings at all times to avoid danger. Say: "i-Buddy and his cousin Jungle Buddy will guide you through these activities to help you learn what to look out for and what to do if you see danger while 'on safari' in Cyberspace."

Have students complete the rest of the page according to the implementation format you have chosen.

Going on Safari Answer Key

Ask the following questions. (Students' answers will vary.)

- How will you travel in the jungle? (Various answers: jeep, truck, land rover, walk, etc.)
- Will it be safer to go alone or with others? (Safer with others.)
- What kinds of dangers do you think you need to watch out for in the jungle? (Wild animals, getting lost, etc.)
- You have decided to hire a guide to help keep you from danger on the safari. What kinds of things do you want your guide to know? (His way around, the good places to go.)
- How will you communicate with others back home to tell them about your travels? (Telephone, write letters.)
- Now think about an online safari. Think about how this kind of journey is similar to a real safari. (Students' answers will vary.)
- How will you travel in Cyberspace? (On the Internet, use a mouse, with assistance from adults.)
- Will it be safer to go alone or with others? (Safer with others.)
- What kinds of dangers do you think you need to watch out for in Cyberspace? (Answers will vary.)
- How will you communicate with others to tell them about your travels? (E-mail, instant messaging.)

Online Extension

Now let's take an online safari! Make sure an adult guide is with you!

The first stop is the Nashville Zoo Web site at http://www.nashvillezoo.org/animals_detail.asp?animalID=57.

Read about the Blue Poison Arrow Frog. *Think safety:* It's safe for us to learn from this Web site. You can find out all about animals without ever leaving your computer.

The next stop is the MeerKat Safari at http://www.meerkatsadventures.com/?gclid=CNPJ_-3h05wCFchW2godAXrNKQ.

This Web site has "links" that can take you to other pages. You are on the main menu page.

1. Click on the picture of the meerkat on the left side or the words that say "What's a meerkat anyway?" This is called a link. It takes you to a page that tells all about meerkats. *Think safety:* This is a safe page where you can read about meerkats.

2. Go back to the main menu. The next link below is a picture of a pink flamingo and words that say "MeerKat Safari's soundtrack." You can click on another link that allows you to listen to a song. The link says "Listen to the MP3 now." *Think safety:* Always ask an adult before clicking on a link that says "listen" or "download now." It could be unsafe. Adults have checked this link so it's OK! Listen to the music!

3. Go back to the main menu page. Now go to the right side of the page and click on the link that is a picture of a lion. It says "Fun animal facts." *Think safety:* This page is safe. You can read interesting things about animals.

4. Go back to the main menu page and click on the link that says "Take home a souvenir." Look where it takes you—it is an online store. *Think safety:* If you see things for sale on the Internet, you must ask an adult to look at the page with you. It is NOT safe to click on items that are for sale. The store may save information about you that you don't want them to have.

5. Go back to the main page and read the information at the bottom of the page. This page also wants you to buy something—a book. *Think safety:* What's the safety rule you just learned? Right—don't buy anything without an adult's help.

The last stop on our safari is the San Diego Zoo's Kid Territory Games at http://www.sandiegozoo.org/kids/games/index.html. *Think safety:* Make sure you have an adult check any game Web site that you visit BEFORE you start playing a game. This is a safe site. The San Diego Zoo has a very safe Web site for kids.

2.2. Safety in the Community (page 4l)

Discuss the meaning of "community" and what it means to be a citizen. Go over the six Safari Citizenship Rules.

Compare the real community to the cyber community. Here's a possible discussion topic listing:

- Explain that when people go into Cyberspace they need to depend on people they know to help keep them safe.
- The main way for children to stay safe on the Internet is to ask for the help of an adult.
- At school when you need help or have a question, who do you ask?
- Who do you ask for help at home?

AUP Tip: Use this activity as reinforcement for your school's acceptable use policy (AUP) by reinforcing who will help students at school when they use computers and/or go on the Internet.

Cyber Citizenship Rules Answer Key

Answers will vary.

Rule 1

This rule should relate to identifying an adult (or "guide") to help use the Internet safely. This may be a parent, teacher, or other trusted adult.

Rule 2

This rule should relate to asking an adult when needing help using the Internet.

Rule 3

This rule should relate to NOT talking to strangers on the Internet. *Note:* This topic will be covered in later activities.

Rule 4

As in Rule 2, this rule should relate to asking an adult when needing help using the Internet.

Rule 5

This rule should relate either to treating people kindly when communicating online or to treating people kindly when using computers.

Rule 6

This rule should relate to getting help from an adult if someone is not following Rule 5.

2.3. Jungle Sights and Online Sites (page 45)

Review the terms "appropriate" and "inappropriate" and have students circle the things that are inappropriate to do on a safari. (Feed a lion, pet a snake, go past the "do not enter" sign.)

Continue the comparison of the real community to the cyber community by relating inappropriate Web sites as not suitable for kids.

KEY POINT: Sometimes people get lost (get to the wrong sites) in Cyberspace. It's not their fault! Have students write about what they would do if they got lost in Cyberspace. Explain that they use a back button or arrow or click on the X to get out of an inappropriate Web site.

Apply It!
Answer Key

Students apply the cyber citizenship rules created on page 43 to answer the questions. Answers will vary.

2.4. Safety Tips (page 49)

Introduces the concept of anonymity online and provides five general Internet safety tips. In the Apply It!, students draw themselves following one of the tips.

2.5. E-mail Safety (page 51)

This section describes e-mail and instant messaging and includes a series of multiple-choice questions and a section for creating e-mail safety tips.

Answer Key

1–B; 2–C; 3–B; 4–C; 5–A

Safety tips should include:

- Ask an adult for help when using e-mail.
- Do not communicate via e-mail with strangers.
- Never write to someone who makes you feel uncomfortable.
- Do not give out personal information.

2.6. Safari Health Check (page 53)

Students learn about computer viruses.

2.7. Learn About Attachments (page 54)

Students learn that attachments may contain computer viruses. Reinforce the idea that adults should help with attachments. Have students circle the area in the e-mail from i-Buddy where an attachment would appear.

2.8. Community Crossword Puzzle (page 56)

The crossword puzzle includes words relating to communities, both real and in Cyberspace.

Answer Key

Across	Down
3. visit	1. Internet
5. address	2. library
7. logon	4. superhighway
8. Web site	6. url
9. community	9. citizen
10. Cyberspace	

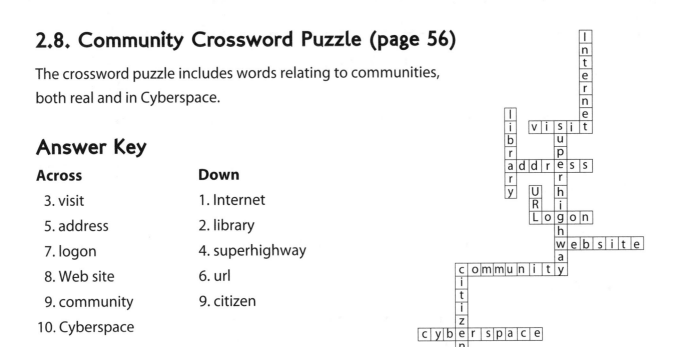

2.9. Apply What You Have Learned Mini-Book (page 57)

Includes instructions for completing the mini-book.

Reach Out to Others

Encourage students to share what they have learned in this unit with others in their families.

GROUP EMPOWERMENT
ACTIVITY

Use the Online Safari theme to have students create a bulletin board to demonstrate Internet safety tips/messages.

 Materials: Bulletin board materials such as construction paper, paint, markers, etc.

Instructions

- As a class, have students brainstorm Internet safety tips learned in this unit.
- Create a title for the bulletin board, such as "Online Cyberspace Safari."
- Assign each student or student group a section of the board.
- Create a background for the bulletin board that depicts the students' ideas of an online safari.
- Embellish with people, animals, computers, Internet places/Web sites, etc., created by the student groups.
- *Optional:* Take a picture of your bulletin board. Send with school name and class information to teachers@isafe.org. Your board might be included in future curriculum materials.

Post-Assessment Reminder

If you will end the i-SAFE program with this unit, have students complete the post-assessments online at http://www.isafe.org/activitybook.

Students complete the Outcomes assessment three to six weeks after completion of the last i-SAFE lesson implemented.

Learning Outcome Evaluation

Review individual worksheets and evaluate each individual's contribution to the group empowerment activity for evidence of concept awareness, general understanding of concept, and concept mastery. Provide continued Internet safety education with materials at levels based on this evaluation.

UNIT 2: ONLINE SAFARI (2–4)
STUDENT PAGES
2.1. GOING ON SAFARI

 Learn About It

Traveling in the online community can be a lot like going on safari. You can explore places you've never been before, but you need to be careful too. You need to be aware of your surroundings at all times to avoid danger. i-Buddy and his cousin Jungle Buddy will guide you through these activities to help you learn what to look out for and what to do if you see danger while "on safari" in Cyberspace.

 Read It

We usually think of our community as the area where we live, which contains places where we know real people. We find places in the community by their addresses, which usually contain a street number and street name. The Internet, also called Cyberspace, is also a community that contains places to visit, just like in the real community. A place in Cyberspace is called a Web site, and it has an address too, called an URL. Every time you are on a Web site, you can see its URL at the top of the screen.

Address | www. | Go

There are communities and places to visit all over the world, but traveling to foreign lands can take some time. The great thing about Cyberspace is that you can travel anywhere with a few clicks of a mouse.

 Apply It!

Let's Go on Safari!

Let's say you are going on safari in the jungle. Write short answers to the following questions.

How will you travel in the jungle?

_____

_____

Will it be safer to go alone or with others?

_____

_____

What kinds of dangers do you think you need to watch out for in the jungle?

_____

_____

You have decided to hire a guide to help keep you from danger on the safari. What kinds of things do you want your guide to know?

_____

_____

How will you communicate with others back home to tell them about your travels?

_____

_____

HELL!!!

Now think about an online safari.

Think about how this kind of journey is like a real safari.

How will you travel in Cyberspace?

_____

_____

Will it be safer to go alone or with others?

_____

_____

What kinds of dangers do you think you need to watch out for in Cyberspace?

_____

_____

How will you communicate with others to tell them about your travels?

_____

_____

Words to Know—You'll need to know the meanings of these words as we go along. Write any other new words you learn here too.

Cyberspace—the Internet

Safari—a journey or expedition

Aware—know about; be informed

Surroundings—that which is all around you

Appropriate—suitable; good for you

Inappropriate—not suitable; not good for you; unsafe

Online Extension

Now let's take an online safari! Make sure an adult guide is with you!

The first stop is the Nashville Zoo Web site at http://www.nashvillezoo.org/animals_detail.asp?animalID=57.

Read about the Blue Poison Arrow Frog. *Think safety:* It's safe for us to learn from this Web site. You can find out all about animals without ever leaving your computer.

The next stop is the MeerKat Safari at http://www.meerkatsadventures.com/?gclid=CNPJ_-3h05wCFchW2godAXrNKQ.

This Web site has "links" that can take you to other pages. You are on the main menu page.

1. Click on the picture of the meerkat on the left side or the words that say "What's a meerkat anyway?" This is called a link. It takes you to a page that tells all about meerkats. *Think safety:* This is a safe page where you can read about meerkats.

2. Go back to the main menu. The next link below is a picture of a pink flamingo and words that say "MeerKat Safari's soundtrack." You can click on another link that allows you to listen to a song. The link says "Listen to the MP3 now." *Think safety:* Always ask an adult before clicking on a link that says "listen" or "download now." It could be unsafe. Adults have checked this link so it's OK! Listen to the music!

3. Go back to the main menu page. Now go to the right side of the page and click on the link that is a picture of a lion. It says "Fun animal facts." *Think safety:* This page is safe. You can read interesting things about animals.

4. Go back to the main menu page and click on the link that says "Take home a souvenir." Look where it takes you—it is an online store. *Think safety:* If you see things for sale on the Internet, you must ask an adult to look at the page with you. It is NOT safe to click on items that are for sale. The store may save information about you that you don't want them to have.

5. Go back to the main page and read the information at the bottom of the page. This page also wants you to buy something—a book. *Think safety:* What's the safety rule you just learned? Right—don't buy anything without an adult's help.

The last stop on our safari is the San Diego Zoo's Kid Territory Games at http://www.sandiegozoo.org/kids/games/index.html. *Think safety:* Make sure you have an adult check any game Web site that you visit BEFORE you start playing a game. This is a safe site. The San Diego Zoo has a very safe Web site for kids.

 ## Learn About It

Community

Community means the place you live, like your neighborhood or town, but the word "community" also has another meaning. A "community" is also made up of people who have something in common with each other. Do you belong to any clubs, sports teams, or church groups? These groups are communities of people who get together because they have the same interest.

A "citizen" is a member of the community; either the community as in "place," like your neighborhood or town, or the community "group" you may belong to.

Rules for Citizens

One reason for rules is to help keep citizens healthy and safe. For example, parents might make a rule about what time a child needs to go to bed so that he or she won't be too tired to think clearly in school.

Safari Safety

Before leaving on safari, your guide says he's got some Safari Citizenship Rules to follow to help everyone enjoy the trip and stay safe.

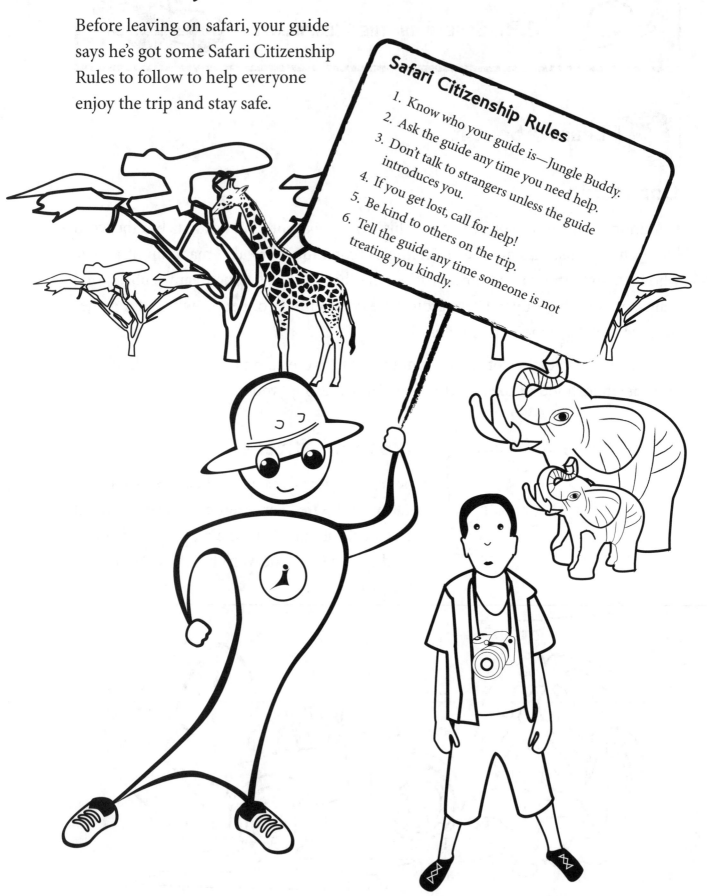

Safari Citizenship Rules

1. Know who your guide is—Jungle Buddy.
2. Ask the guide any time you need help.
3. Don't talk to strangers unless the guide introduces you.
4. If you get lost, call for help!
5. Be kind to others on the trip.
6. Tell the guide any time someone is not treating you kindly.

Apply It!

How can you learn from the Safari Citizenship Rules to make online travel safer?
Use each safari rule on page 42 to make an Internet use rule for cyber citizens.
Hint: first decide who your real-life "guide" will be for using the Internet. Will it be
your parent or parents, or a teacher?

Cyber Citizenship Rules

Rule 1

_____

_____

_____

Rule 2

_____

_____

_____

Rule 3

_____

_____

_____

Rule 4

_____

_____

_____

Rule 5

_____

_____

_____

Rule 6

_____

_____

_____

2.3. JUNGLE SIGHTS . . . AND

On a jungle safari there are lots of sights to see. There are fun things to do and things that will help us learn—we call these "appropriate" (they are good for us).

Sometimes you might come across something that is just too scary or dangerous, or even against the law to do. These are "inappropriate" for this trip! Stay away from these types of things, they are unsafe for us.

Circle the scenes below that are inappropriate to do on a safari.

 • Feed a lion

 • Pet a poisonous snake

 • Observe an unusual flower

 • Explore a cave with the guide

 • Go past a DO NOT ENTER sign

  • Take pictures of monkeys

On the Internet there are lots of appropriate (good for you) "sites" to see—Web sites that is!

Web sites that are not suitable for kids are called "inappropriate." These kinds of Web sites might be scary, dangerous, or even against the law to go to! Good cyber citizens go to appropriate places and stay away from inappropriate places.

Think of your favorite place on the Internet. Is it a game or a site about a celebrity or TV show?

Write It Here

_____

_____

_____

_____

_____

_____

Lost in Cyberspace

Can you get lost in Cyberspace? YES!

Sometimes people get lost on the Internet, and go to inappropriate Web sites by mistake.

It's not their fault—it happens by mistake!

Unsafe Internet sites (to stay away from!)

Unsafe Web sites might:

- Ask you to tell all about yourself
- Ask for money
- Say mean things about people
- Tell about hurting people

On Safari you need to be prepared!

What do you do if you get lost? *Hint:* Look back at the safari rules.

Write your answer here:

_____

_____

_____

_____

_____

_____

_____

_____

On the Internet you need to be prepared!

> Any Web site that doesn't make sense to you is inappropriate, and it can be unsafe.

 ## Apply It!

Think about the cyber citizenship rules you came up with in an earlier activity.

Apply your rules here

What will you do if you get to an unsafe Web site?

First I would try:

_____

_____

_____

_____

If that didn't work, I would:

_____

_____

_____

_____

> Go BACK to get out of appropriate Web sites—click on the back arrow or right click and choose "Back."
>
> ## X it out to EXIT.
>
> Exit Web sites you don't want to be in by clicking on the X in the top right corner of your screen (webpage) or by Xing out tabs.

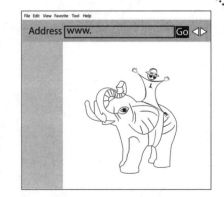

2.4. SAFETY TIPS

 Learn About It

If you were on a real safari, you would know everyone in your group (the community—remember?), you would be able to see them, and your parents would know them too. But it's different when you are exploring in Cyberspace. You can't usually see people, and even if you do see them, you can't be sure who they are. People you don't know (strangers) have ways of sending you messages and asking you to tell about yourself on the Internet. An important thing to remember is that people on the Internet don't always tell the truth.

There are tips to help you remember how to keep yourself safe while traveling in Cyberspace.

1. Never give out personal information such as your name, home address, school name, telephone number, or your picture on the Internet without your parents' permission.

2. Never write to someone on the Internet who has made you feel uncomfortable or scared.

3. Do not meet someone or have him or her visit you without the permission of your parents.

4. Tell your parents or a trusted adult right away if you read anything on the Internet that makes you feel bad or uncomfortable.

5. Remember that people online may not be who they say they are.

Apply It!

Draw a picture of yourself following one of the safety tips and write the tip below the picture.

_____

_____

_____

_____

 **2.5. E-mail Safety**

 ## Learn About It

If you were on a safari trip and wanted to tell other people about it, you would have to either call them on the phone or send a letter. It's much easier to communicate on the Internet!

One way is IM (Instant Messaging).

Do you IM?

Another way is by e-mail. E-mail is a great way to communicate with someone you and your parents know. An e-mail is a letter that is sent over the Internet. Instead of going to your street address like a real letter, it goes to an "e-mail address" on the Internet. To send an e-mail, you write your letter on the computer and click SEND! You can send an e-mail to anyone who has an e-mail address. Even if you don't use e-mail yet, it's important to know about it.

Multiple-Choice Review

Circle the letter of the correct answer to each question.

1. Does everybody tell the truth on the Internet?

   A. Yes

   B. No

2. Which one of these is personal information?

   A. Your dog's name

   B. A movie you like

   C. Your street address

3. What should you do if someone in Cyberspace is making you feel uncomfortable?

   A. Send the person an e-mail

   B. Tell an adult about it right away

   C. Think about it tomorrow

4. What is a URL?

   A. A Web site about safety

   B. Your street address

   C. A Web site's address

5. What does "inappropriate" mean?

   A. Not good for someone

   B. E-mail addresses

   C. Places your parents let you go to

 ## Apply It!

Read the safety tips from page 49 again and think about them. Then use what you learned from them to create two or three safety tips about using e-mail.

1 _____

_____

_____

_____

2 _____

_____

_____

_____

3 _____

_____

_____

_____

2.6. SAFARI HEALTH CHECK

Learn About It

Everyone on this safari needs to take steps to prevent illness. There are all kinds of illnesses and viruses out there. What's a virus? A virus is a germ that can make you sick. And some viruses can be spread from one person to another. We don't want any sick people ruining our trip!

One way you can get a virus in the jungle is to get infected by a bug bite.

Online Health Check

Do you know? Computers can get viruses too, but they don't catch them from people's germs! Read about computer viruses in the next section. If you are not sure of the meaning of any words, circle them.

A computer virus is really a type of computer program. A computer program is what makes the computer do things. A computer game is a program—a good kind of computer program. A computer virus is a very bad kind of computer program. It makes the computer sick. It destroys good programs and sometimes makes the computer stop working. Sometimes it just does strange things, like make good programs disappear or not work right. A virus can ruin a computer.

Other names for computer viruses are:

- Worms
- Trojan horses

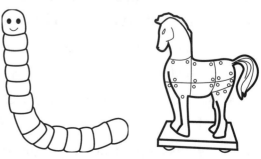

2.7. Learn About Attachments

Sometimes e-mail arrives with an extra message or picture attached to it. They are called "attachments."

It's fun to look at things like pictures, but you need to check with an adult before you open an e-mail attachment because sometimes strangers attach computer viruses to e-mails! Then they send them out to make people's computers sick! The viruses hide in the e-mail attachment.

Think About It

What do you think about somebody who would send a hidden virus to another person's computer in an e-mail? Would a good citizen do this?"

Sending a computer virus on purpose is really just the same as trying to break a computer with a hammer! And there are laws against it. A person can go to jail for making a virus and sending it to other people!

Find It!

Look on the next page at the e-mail from i-Buddy. Find and circle the area on this e-mail message where you would see an attachment.

Safety Tips

The best way to keep your computer from catching a virus is to ask your parents or another adult to help you when you open up e-mail. And even when your parents do help you, don't open up or click on an e-mail that has an attachment unless your parents were expecting to receive it. You can always use the phone to call the person who sent the e-mail, to make sure the attachment is safe before you open it. You will be a hero for your whole family if you prevent a virus from attacking your computer!

NO VIRUSES

Look! It is an e-mail message from i-Buddy.

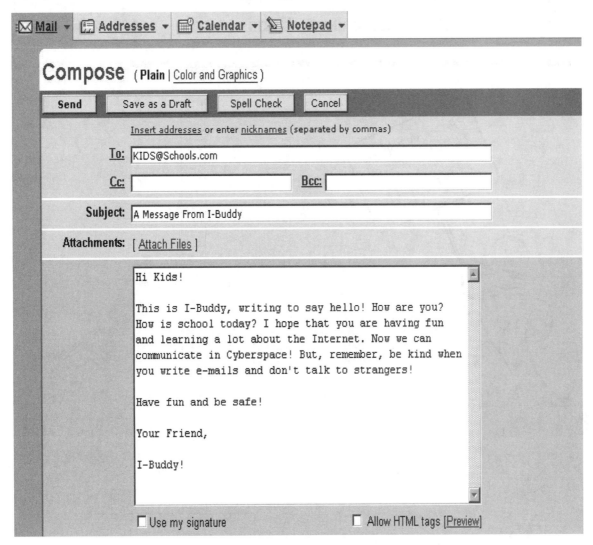

Mail ▾ | **Addresses** ▾ | **Calendar** ▾ | **Notepad** ▾

Compose (**Plain** | Color and Graphics)

| Send | Save as a Draft | Spell Check | Cancel |

Insert addresses or enter nicknames (separated by commas)

To: KIDS@Schools.com

Cc: [ ] **Bcc:** [ ]

Subject: A Message From I-Buddy

Attachments: [Attach Files]

Hi Kids!

This is I-Buddy, writing to say hello! How are you?
How is school today? I hope that you are having fun
and learning a lot about the Internet. Now we can
communicate in Cyberspace! But, remember, be kind when
you write e-mails and don't talk to strangers!

Have fun and be safe!

Your Friend,

I-Buddy!

☐ Use my signature   ☐ Allow HTML tags [Preview]

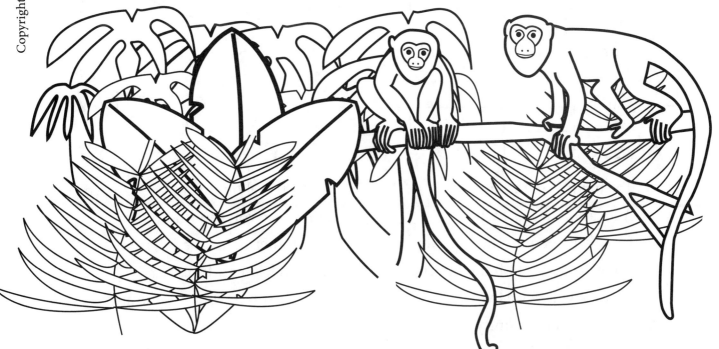

2.8. COMMUNITY CROSSWORD

Hi, can you help me with the Community Puzzle? GIVE IT A TRY!

Across

3. To stop in somewhere
5. A location has its own _____
7. How you get onto the Internet
8. A place you visit on the Internet
9. An area where we live
10. An online community

Down

1. We travel on this in Cyberspace
2. A place you can find books
4. Another name for Internet
6. A Web site's address
9. A person in your community

56 Unit 2: Online Safari (2–4)

 # Wrap-Up_Apply It!

Make a mini-book to show what you have learned.

Instructions: Use the last two pages of this packet and fold them together to make a mini-book:

- Fold the first page in half so that the cover is on top
- Fold the second page in half so that the page labeled "Page 2" is on top.
- Place the second folded page inside the first folded page to make a mini-book.
- Staple the folded edge if desired.

Color the cover and write your name on it.

Page 1

These are all places that make up a community or neighborhood. These are places where we know real people.

- Draw and label a place you like to go in your community.

Page 2

Think about your class at school. Are you a community?

Yes, you are. As students, you have the same grade level in common, have the same teacher, and have other things in common. You are a community. You communicate with each other about, and participate in, the same school activities. People in a community are called citizens.

- Draw or write your ideas of a place you like to go in Cyberspace.

Page 3

- Write a rule that you follow to stay safe and to be a good citizen.

Page 4

There are community laws and rules made by your parents, which keep you safe from inappropriate places in the community. Good citizens go to appropriate places and stay away from inappropriate places.

- Read the list of words. Circle the places that are appropriate for kids. Put an X over the places that are inappropriate and unsafe for kids.

Page 5

- Read the sentence starter.
- Write down, and/or draw a picture of, what you would do if you entered an inappropriate Web site by mistake.

Page 6

You have learned that there are different communities, including the local community and the cyber community, and that a good citizen makes smart decisions. A good citizen is a responsible citizen.

- Give an example of something you know to do to show that you are a good cyber citizen.

Reach Out to Others!

Take your booklet home and share what you have learned with others in your family.

i-Buddy Presents

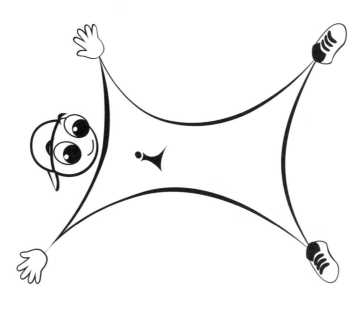

Community & Citizenship, Cyber Community & Ciber Citizens

I am the key to building a safer USA

NAME: _____

I like to go _____

in my community

- ✂

- ✂

I would get out of an

inapropiate Web site by...

A responsible Cyber Citizen Knows...

_____

_____

_____

_____

And...Cyber Smart means Cyber Safe!

Directions: Circle the appropiate places. Place an X over the places that are inapropiate for you.

Library

"R" rated movie

Restaurant

A stranger's house

Police station   A bar

School   A friend's house

Grocery store

I am a citizen

3

I am safe in my community
when I follow these rules:

4

Unit 3: Heroes Against Cyber Bullying (3–4)

Unit Goal

Throughout the lesson/activities, learners will begin to develop an understanding of the need to make responsible choices, beginning with always having an adult's help when going on-line, to ensure personal safety. Students will engage in a group discussion moderated by the teacher to (a) provide exposure to vocabulary words related to the Internet and (b) gain a basic awareness of a comparison of the physical community to the abstract concept of Cyberspace as a community.

Understanding the Unit Format

This guide will provide you with discussion guidance, answers to activity questions, and explanations of the content of the student pages. Where applicable, this guide will also provide tips for reinforcing your acceptable use policies (AUP) with the activity concepts.

Heroes Against Cyber Bullying lesson/activity sections include:

3.1. Heroes Against Cyber Bullying

3.2. What Is a Hero?

3.3. Sticks and Stones

3.4. Kind vs. Unkind

3.5. Getting the Bigger Picture—Cyberspace as a Global Community

3.6. Tips to End Cyber Bullying

3.7. Write a Cyber Tale

Additional Resources

Refer to the i-SAFE *i-EDUCATOR Times* newsletters located at www.isafe.org and general i-SAFE lesson plans on similar topics for additional resource materials and background information if needed.

Prepare for the Lesson

Pre-Assessment

- If beginning the i-SAFE program with this unit, administer the pre-assessment online at http://www.isafe.org/activitybook.
- Enter School ID# 24615.

Post-Assessment

- If you will end the i-SAFE program with this unit, have students complete the post-assessment online at http://www.isafe.org/activitybook.
- Students complete the Outcomes assessment three to six weeks after completion of the last i-SAFE lesson implemented.

Plan Your Format

This unit is designed to enable transition from traditional class lessons to a more self-guided format, depending on student reading abilities.

1. Arrange for students to take the online pre-assessment.
2. Review the student activity pages and determine how you will implement the unit.
3. *Optional:* Prepare any additional reference material of your choice, including Internet access.
4. Provide each student with a copy of the student pages and review directions for student use.

Implementation Options

The following are suggested options for implementing the unit.

Group guided: Use the activities as short lessons over a period of time (one or two weeks to complete). This option is especially recommended for students with less developed reading comprehension skills.

- Have students complete the online pre-assessment prior to engaging in the i-SAFE program.
- Assign and go over each activity page with the class as a large group and have students complete them as instructed. You may want to have students read over text parts together to reinforce meaning.
- Go over completed pages with the group as they are finished.
- Have students complete the online post-assessment.
- Complete the empowerment activity suggested, or create your own activity.

Small groups: Students work in groups to complete the activities. This may be done in several sessions.

- Have students complete the online pre-assessment prior to engaging in the i-SAFE program.
- Introduce the unit with the pre-activity discussion.
- Create small work groups of three to four students.

- Student groups complete the assigned pages for each session and discuss their answers within the group.
- Go over the Wrap-Up activity to review the concepts presented in the unit.
- Have students complete the online post-assessment.
- Complete the empowerment activity suggested, or create your own activity.

Semi-self-guided: This option should only be considered for age-proficient readers. Create a timeline for activities to be completed.

- Have students complete the online pre-assessment prior to engaging in the i-SAFE program.
- Introduce the unit with the Activity 1 discussion.
- Have students complete their assignments.
- Go over the Wrap-Up activity to review the concepts.
- Have students complete the online post-assessment.
- Complete the empowerment activity suggested, or create your own activity.

3.1. Heroes Against Cyber Bullying (page 73)

Go over "Learn About It" at the top of the first page to introduce the unit: Going online can be like exploring a whole new world. Sometimes we can forget that the online environment has rules. We might take risks, say and do things we wouldn't normally do, because we feel safe and sheltered behind the computer screen. But it's important to remember that isn't true—there are consequences for our actions, even online.

Vocabulary check: It is important that students understand the meaning of "consequences."

Have students complete the rest of the page according to the implementation format you have chosen.

Answer Key

Apply It!

(Student answers should reflect and reinforce your school's safety rules.)

Think About the Online World. (Student answers should reflect school acceptable use policies for technology use.)

AUP Tip: Use this activity as reinforcement for your school's acceptable use policy (AUP) by reinforcing who will help them at school when they use computers and/or go on the Internet.

Option: Make a Survey

Help students learn that cyber bullying affects most students. Using the instructions on page 75, help students create and conduct a survey about online behavior.

The survey can be done on a larger scale by posting the questions in a more public place in the school, such as the library, and providing a box for students to submit their answers.

Discuss reasons why it is easy for Internet users to forget that there are rules online. Discussion should reflect the concepts surrounding the inability to see how others react when online.

3.2. What Is a Hero? (page 77)

Students answer questions that define and conceptualize what a hero is. The concept is then applied to thinking about online experiences.

Implementation Note: it is important for children in this age group to understand that being a "hero" when it comes to helping themselves or those who are victimized is the ideal every cyber citizen should strive for.

Vocabulary Check

Students define the following words:

rule

citizenship

courage

hero

bully

3.3. Sticks and Stones (page 80)

Students are asked to respond to how they feel about the statement "Sticks and stones can break my bones, but words will never hurt me" and to give an example of something that would hurt their own or their friends' feelings. Students then brainstorm rules to be good citizens online. The rules should reflect class and school rules of behavior as well as unique rules that apply to netiquette. For example:

- Treat others online as you expect to be treated.
- Use meaningful subject lines. Tell people what you are sending to them so they know what to expect when the message is opened.
- Don't type with ALL CAPS. This is known as online screaming, and it is considered to be rude.
- Think before you type. E-mails are not like spoken words; they do not go away after you say them.
- Because what you write is more permanent, you must be very careful about what you say and how you say it. Once you hit "send," you have no control over the message! It's easy to be misunderstood in Cyberspace because you can't see the other person face-to-face. Be clear about what you want to say.
- Don't send a message when you are angry. It's hard to undo things that are said in anger.
- Think about attachments in e-mail and IMs. Don't send something as an attachment unless you really need to. Don't send really large attachments. Don't send attachments with viruses. And . . . be careful of attachments you download.
- Don't Spam. Don't send out messages that aren't wanted!

3.4. Kind vs. Unkind (page 81)

Use this section to reinforce that kindness online is an important attribute. Students should reflect on how they feel if bullied or treated unkindly.

3.5. Getting the Bigger Picture—Cyberspace as a Global Community (page 81)

Fill in each blank with one or more words to create a concept of how cyber bullying affects more than just the individuals involved. Possible answers:

The Internet connects people **around** the world with the ability to communicate. They do this with words through **e-mail and text messaging** and with pictures or video on Web sites such as **YouTube**. In Europe and the United Kingdom, youth started an activity called "happy slapping," in which someone would take a cell phone video of someone being attacked and then post it on the Internet. People of all ages **around the** world were able to **see and share** these videos. It didn't take long for people in other parts of the world to do their own happy slapping.

1. List ways this example shows that Cyberspace is a "global community." Possible answers:

   - The internet connects people from around the world.
   - Something that a person posts in a foreign country such as England or the Germany can be seen in any other country.
   - People on the Internet use all the different languages of the world.
   - Children all over the world can view videos, even TV shows, from other countries.

2. Happy slapping is a negative (unkind) action and has a negative (bad) impact on the societies where it happens. Create a scenario that shows a way to use the Internet to cause positive (good) changes in societies.

   Sample answers:

   - The Internet has been used for many positive changes in society. For example:
     - People use the Internet to post petitions for signatures to make changes on hot topics and to garner support for a cause.
     - People use the Internet as a means of creating support environments to bring people together and share in ways that allow for new information to emerge, such as for medical diseases.
     - People use the Internet to promote new ideas/inventions, resulting in new products to market that make a difference in society.

Online Extension Teacher Resource

With the Internet it's easy for students to connect with others from around the world. The hardest part is ensuring that the activity, method, and means for doing so are safe and secure for the students. In addition to the Web site featured in the online extension for students (Kids' Space Connection at http://www.ks-connection.org/), the site www.epals.com allows teachers to advertise, search for, and select "online pen pals" in classrooms around the world. The site focuses on projects and topics that the e-pals collaborate on. The project helps teachers match up with other classrooms around the world on a topic of interest and ensure that the exchange is safe and secure. Take the time to register your class and allow them to see how the Internet can bring people from around the world together.

3.6. Tips to End Cyber Bullying (page 84)

Gives students ways to prevent and respond to cyber bullying.

3.7. Write a Cyber Tale (page 86)

Students use what they now know about cyber bullying to write a story that includes the following:

1. A cyber bullying problem
2. How the bully and victim acted
3. A positive (good) solution that helps the victim
4. A "consequence" for the cyber bully

End with a tip to let others know how to be safe from cyber bullies.

Use this activity to evaluate the concepts students have learned.

Evaluation

1. Has a realistic cyber bullying problem been identified?
2. The story should reflect both sides of the problem. Does the story clearly identify what the bully did? Does the victim do anything to perpetuate the problem?
3. Evaluate the solution. Does it conform to class/school rules? Does it conform to the basic rule of "tell a trusted adult"?
4. What kind of consequence does the bully face? Has the author included how the bully felt?
5. Has the author illustrated a realistic tip for preventing cyber bullying?

Group Empowerment Activity Ideas

- Use the stories created to build a big book or "Internet Safety" library to share and demonstrate what they have learned.
- Have students read their stories to younger children in the school.
- Assign students to read their stories to siblings at home and write short reports on the experience.

Post-Assessment Reminder

If you will end the i-SAFE program with this unit, have students complete the post-assessments online at http://www.isafe.org/activitybook.

Students complete the Outcomes assessment three to six weeks after completion of the last i-SAFE lesson implemented.

3.1 Heroes Against Cyber Bullying

Learn About It

Going online can be like exploring a whole new world. Sometimes we can forget that the online environment has rules. We might take risks, say and do things we wouldn't normally do because we feel safe and sheltered behind the computer screen. But it's important to remember that isn't true. There are consequences for our actions, even online.

Vocabulary Check

Consequences: Something that logically happens after an action or condition. For example, if a ball is thrown at a glass window, the "consequence" may be a broken window.

Apply It!

List two possible "consequences" of following a school safety rule.

1. _____

_____

_____

2. _____

_____

_____

List two possible "consequences" of breaking a school safety rule.

1. _____

_____

_____

2. _____

_____

_____

Think About the Online World

List two possible "consequences" of following a rule for school Internet or computer use.

1. _____

_____

_____

2. _____

_____

_____

List two possible "consequences" of breaking a rule for school Internet or computer use.

1. _____

   _____

   _____

2. _____

   _____

   _____

Read It

There are many reasons to remember that there are rules and consequences to our online actions. Rules help keep things orderly and friendly and help to make sure that no one gets hurt. However, it seems that online rules are often ignored.

One survey of 1,500 students in fourth through eighth grade found that 42 percent (almost half) had been bullied online. And 53 percent (more than half) admitted that they had said something mean or hurtful to someone else online.

Option: Make a Survey

Work with a small group of classmates to make a survey about the ways kids act online. Create two or three questions such as:

- Have you ever sent a mean IM, text message, or e-mail to someone?

  Yes   No

- Has anyone ever sent a mean IM, text message, or e-mail to you?

  Yes   No

- Do you know someone who has done something to another person using the Internet?

  Yes   No

Conduct the survey. Write the questions you have created on the board and have each person in the class write his or her answers on a small piece of paper. Explain that it is very important that they answer the questions honestly. Do not have them put their names on the papers. Collect the papers, mix them up, and tally up the answers and share the results with the class.

> You can do the survey on a larger scale by posting the questions in a more public place in the school, such as the library, and providing a box for students to submit their answers.

List at least three reasons why it is easy for Internet users to forget that there are rules online.

1. _____
   _____
   _____

2. _____
   _____
   _____

3. _____
   _____
   _____

3.2. What Is a Hero?

What does courage have to do with being a hero?

_____

_____

_____

_____

What kinds of things do heroes do?

_____

_____

_____

_____

Heroes Can Be Everyday People Too!

Do you know somebody in real life who has acted like a hero? (For example: standing up for someone, doing something difficult, or going out of his or her way to help someone.)

_____

_____

_____

_____

_____

What did this hero do?

_____

_____

_____

_____

_____

_____

It's important to remember that little things can make anyone a hero!

Unit 3: Heroes Against Cyber Bullying (3–4) 77

Now Think About an Online Hero

Can someone be a hero online?

_____

_____

_____

_____

How? Give an example.

_____

_____

_____

_____

_____

Vocabulary Check

Words to know: Write the meaning of each word below.

Rule: _____

_____

_____

_____

_____

Citizenship: _____

_____

_____

_____

_____

Courage: _____

_____

_____

_____

_____

Hero: _____

_____

_____

_____

_____

Bully: _____

_____

_____

_____

_____

3.3. Sticks and Stones

 Think About It

Think about the following saying:

Sticks and stones may break my bones, but words can never hurt me.

Do you think that is true? Why or why not?

_____

_____

_____

Write an example of something that would hurt your, or someone else's feelings.

_____

_____

_____

 Read It

When you "talk" online, the only way you have to express yourself is through your words. People can't see your face to see whether you are laughing or that you are joking. PLUS you can't see the other person's face to see whether you hurt his or her feelings.

Brainstorm rules to be a good citizen online and write them here:

_____

_____

_____

_____

_____

Think About It

In surveys, i-SAFE found 53 percent—that means chances are that either you or the person sitting next to you—said something mean or hurtful online.

Do you think they meant to be cyber bullies? Perhaps not—but we don't always know how our words will affect the person who receives them.

3.4. Kind vs. Unkind

Kindness: To be kind is to be nice to others. Kind acts are helpful, show consideration, and make the givers and the receivers feel good. Kind acts are NOT mean.

You like it when others show kindness to you.

Can you think of an example of when someone was nice to you or considerate of your feelings?

Write it here:

_____

_____

_____

Bullying: When someone is mean to others and picks on them, it's bullying. That includes making fun of others, calling them names, or beating up on them.

Cyber bullying: Cyber bullies are those bullies who use the Internet to knock others down. Texting and e-mail provides easy ways for bullies to be mean to others.

Another way bullies use the Internet is through blogs and chat sites to make their comments public. Finally, some cyber bullies build Web sites or networking pages devoted to making a person or persons feel bad.

> **Kindness can become its own motive.**
> **We are made kind by being kind.** – *Eric Hoffer*

3.5. Getting the Bigger Picture—Cyberspace as a Global Community

Fill in each blank with one or more words to create a concept of how cyber bullying affects more than just the individuals involved.

The Internet connects people _____ the world with the ability to communicate. They do this with words through _____ and with pictures or video on Web sites like _____ . In Europe and the United Kingdom, youth started an activity called "happy slapping," in which someone would take a cell phone video of someone being attacked and then post it on the Internet. People of all ages world were able to _____ these videos. It didn't take long for people in other parts of the world to do their own happy slapping.

Answer the following:

1. List ways this example shows that Cyberspace is a "global community."

_____

_____

_____

_____

_____

_____

2. Happy slapping is a negative (unkind) action and has a negative (bad) impact on the societies where it happens. Create a scenario that shows a way to use the Internet to cause positive (good) changes in societies.

_____

_____

_____

_____

_____

_____

The following are true stories from countries around the world. For each, write your idea of how the incident should be handled.

A teacher created a blog entry making fun of his eight-year-old students and their schoolwork. The blog was discovered and its URL was passed around to other netizens.

EXTRA EXTRA read all about it

_____

_____

_____

_____

A thirteen-year-old girl named Carla was being bullied by two schoolboys who set up a Web site to attack her. Carla was embarrassed and did not tell her parents about the Web site.

_____

_____

_____

_____

Gary got a cell phone for his tenth birthday. After a couple of weeks he started getting mean text messages from a boy named Kent, from his school. At first he ignored it, but he kept getting them and he started to get worried. Kent demanded that Gary meet him after lunch each day and pay him money. That's when Gary decided to delete the messages without telling anyone. Kent threatened Gary by telling him that he would tell their teacher that Gary was bullying him! (Think about it—was it smart for Gary to delete the mean messages?)

_____

_____

_____

_____

3.6. Tips to End Cyber Bullying

No one should put up with bullying!

- **Tell someone.** Don't keep cyber bullying to yourself. If you are bullied or know someone else who is, tell a trusted adult about it. This might be a parent, teacher, friend's parent—even an older brother or sister.
- **Don't open or read messages from cyber bullies.**
- **Tell a teacher** if you receive a bullying message while at school.
- **Don't erase the messages.** They may be needed to take action. Show the messages to a trusted adult.
- **Protect yourself.** Never agree to meet with the person or with anyone you meet online.
- **If you are bullied through chat or IM, the bully can be blocked. Tell someone! He or she will help!**
- **Don't give out private information** online such as passwords, PIN numbers, addresses, or phone numbers. This information can be used by bullies and other harmful people on the Internet.
- **Use netiquette.** Be polite online and others will tend to do the same. If someone does get angry or bullies you, **ignore him or her**—online cyber bullies want a reaction just like other bullies.
- **Don't send a message when you are angry.** It is hard to undo things that are said in anger.
- **When something doesn't seem right, it probably isn't. Get out of the site, chat, etc.**
- **Give people you meet online the same respect you would give someone in person.**

Use Emoticons

Emoticons stand for emotion icons. When e-mailing, IMing, or chatting, writers use emoticons to show when they are joking, upset, or angry. Emoticons help the reader understand what the writer is really trying to say. Use characters on your keyboard to make emoticons. The most common one is the smile. It is used to tell people "Don't take what I said seriously; I meant it as a joke or in good humor." A smile :) can be made with a colon for the eyes, a dash for the nose, and the right parenthesis for the smiling mouth. :-)

Online Extension

Before the Internet, people would make friends from all around the world by writing letters to each other. They were called "pen pals." The Internet has made it much easier to learn about people and make friends anywhere in the world through "e-pals" using e-mail and instant messaging.

If you are going to have an Internet pen pal, however, it is very important to think about safety before making any online friends. The best way to ensure safety is to have an adult help you search for a Web site that builds safety features into its program. One example of a safe site is Kids' Space Connection at http://www.ks-connection.org/. Kids' Space Connection is an international meeting place for children and schoolteachers where you can find pen pals from around the world. The site features projects and cool clubs you can join, too.

Check it out! Go to the link above and click on the link for the "Privacy Policy" at the bottom of the page.

Challenge question: How does this Web site protect its users?

_____

_____

_____

_____

3.7. Write a Cyber Tale

Think about everything you now know about cyber bullying. Write a story that includes the following:

- A cyber bullying problem
- How the bully and victim acted
- A positive (good) solution that helps the victim
- A "consequence" for the cyber bully

End the story with a tip to let others know how to be safe from cyber bullies.

_____

_____

_____

_____

_____

_____

_____

_____

_____

_____

_____

_____

_____

_____

_____

_____

_____

_____

_____

_____

_____

_____

Unit 4: Managing Personal Information Online (5–8)

Unit 4: Managing Personal Information Online (5–8) Teacher's Guide

Unit Goal

Throughout the lesson/activities, learners will develop an understanding of the need to make responsible choices to ensure personal safety.

Understanding the Unit Format

This portion of the unit will provide you with discussion guidance, answers to activity questions, and explanations of the content of the student pages.

Managing Personal Information Online lesson/activity sections include:

4.1. Safeguarding Your Online Identity: Screen Names and Passwords

4.2. Get Real About Online Profiles

4.3. Beyond Revealing Simple Information

4.4. Truths About Online Strangers

4.5. Enrichment Activity—Wrap It Up!

4.6. Unit Review

Additional Resources

Refer to the i-SAFE *i-EDUCATOR Times* newsletters located at www.isafe.org and general i-SAFE lesson plans on similar topics for additional resource materials and background information if needed.

Prepare for the Lesson

Pre-Assessment

- If beginning the i-SAFE program with this unit, administer the pre-assessment online at http://www.isafe.org/activitybook.
- Enter School ID# 24615.

Post-Assessment

- If you will end the i-SAFE program with this unit, have students complete the post-assessment online at http://www.isafe.org/activitybook.

- Students complete the Outcomes assessment three to six weeks after completion of the last i-SAFE lesson implemented.

Plan Your Format

This unit is designed to enable transition from traditional class lessons to a more self-guided format, depending on student reading abilities.

1. Arrange for students to take the online pre-assessment.
2. Review the student activity pages and determine how you will implement the unit.
3. *Optional:* Prepare any additional reference material of your choice, including Internet access.
4. Provide each student with a copy of the student pages and review directions for student use.

Implementation Options

The following are suggested options for implementing the unit.

Group guided: Use the activities as short lessons over a period of time (one or two weeks to complete). This option is especially recommended for students with less developed reading comprehension skills.

- Have students complete the online pre-assessment prior to engaging in the i-SAFE program.
- Assign and go over each activity page with the class as a large group and have students complete them as instructed. You may want to have students read over text parts together to reinforce meaning.
- Go over completed pages with the group as they are finished.
- Have students complete the online post-assessment.
- Complete the empowerment activity suggested, or create your own activity.

Small groups: Students work in groups to complete the activities. This may be done in several sessions.

- Have students complete the online pre-assessment prior to engaging in the i-SAFE program.
- Introduce the unit with the pre-activity discussion.
- Create small work groups of three to four students.
- Student groups complete the assigned pages for each session and discuss their answers within the group.
- Go over the Wrap-Up activity to review the concepts presented in the unit.

- Have students complete the online post-assessment.
- Complete the empowerment activity suggested, or create your own activity.

Semi-self-guided: This option should only be considered for age-proficient readers. Create a timeline for activities to be completed.

- Have students complete the online pre-assessment prior to engaging in the i-SAFE program.
- Introduce the unit with the Activity 1 discussion.
- Have students complete their assignments.
- Go over the Wrap-Up activity to review the concepts.
- Have students complete the online post-assessment.

4.I. Safeguarding Your Online Identity: Screen Names and Passwords (page 102)

To introduce the unit:

- Have a student read the introduction out loud.

- As a class, go over the explanations of the sections in "Understanding the Activities."

- Have students complete the activities according to the implementation format you have chosen.

Definitions of Terms to Know

- **anonymous**—of unknown name

- **appropriate**—suitable or fitting for a particular purpose, person, occasion, etc.

- **identify**—to recognize or establish as being a particular person or thing; verify the identity of

- **inappropriate**—unsuitable or improper

- **non-identifying**—information that is common to many

- **online profile**—Internet posting of one's characteristics or qualities

- **password**—a word or other string of characters, kept secret or confidential, that must be supplied by a user in order to gain full or partial access to a system

- **personal information**—information that describes a person's identity such as name, date of birth, address, etc.

- **random**—proceeding, made, or occurring without definite aim, reason, or pattern

- **screen name**—online nickname or identity

- **user ID**—same as screen name

Use What U Have Learned Answer Key

Contain Identifying (or Potentially Identifying) Information

- andersonMJ (initials and last name)

- Brandonclassof2012 (name and graduation year—tells age)

- carrie_lewis@gmc.net (e-mail address)

- GTaylorplaysGuitar (initial, name, hobby)

- Miamisue13 (name, location, age)
- wellesleygirl (location, gender)

DO NOT Contain Identifying Information
- canarielover
- GerbilsRkewl
- namelessjester9
- nymets29
- REMforever
- rockhound92008

What Do U Think? Answer Key

It is safe to reveal interests or hobbies in screen names as long as that information is not paired with a name or other identifying pieces of information. For example, although some of the screen names listed in the above activity contain potential information about interests or hobbies, they are only unsafe when paired with identifying information.

Online ID—What Can You Tell? Answer Key

1. dancinfun—very general with an idea of a hobby
2. Bayareababe—gives a general location and gender
3. Smithstealshome—gives the last name an idea of a hobby/interest
4. Jessica4dance—gives first name and a favorite activity
5. Fred14—gives first name and probable age

Use What U Have Learned Answer Key

Rule should reflect concept of safety in passwords.
Passwords created should be a random grouping of letters and/or numbers.

Free Write Answer Key

Writing should include examples of dangers involved when others know or guess someone else's password, such as:

- Identity can be stolen.
- Money could be stolen from an online account.
- A Web site or webpage could be deleted or damaged.
- Someone could send e-mail or post messages as another person.

4.2. Get Real About Online Profiles (page 108)

Terms to Know Answer Key

- **enable**—to make possible or easy; to make able
- **online profile**—online posting of personal information (name, age, address, etc.) used to sign up for online services or activities
- **privacy settings**—options or selections that can be made on a Web site that can make an online profile or other information unavailable to the public and/or searchable

Chat Activity Answer Key

The underlined sections indicate the personal information that could lead to identification and location of the chatters.

Darthvader<u>12</u>: Hey what's everyone up to?

Busybee: Not much here. I've been working on math homework.

DianaKleary: Math—that's my favorite subject! LOL!

Tennispro444: Are u nuts girl? Math! I'd rather get my teeth pulled than do math.

Darthvader12: So you're a math whiz Diana—maybe you could help me with my algebra.

DianaKleary: Sure no problem—Darthvader12—what is your real name anyway?

Darthvader12: <u>Bryan</u>

DianaKleary: OK. Now I know U—no problem. I tutor at <u>my school, American International</u>—this is my cell. Ask me ? anytime. <u>443-773-6691</u>.

Busybee: so darth r u like a huge Star Wars fan or something?

Darthvader12: yeah pretty much

SmithinToronto: That is neat. Me, I'm not much into videos. I'd rather listen to music. KWIM?

Busybee: Hey Smith, ?4U—Are you in Toronto? Is it snowing there?

SmithinToronto: <u>I live right across from Air Canada Centre</u>. No snow yet. But its cold!

Tennispro444: I've never seen snow. We don't see much of it in <u>Hawaii</u> lol

Darthvader12: Hawaii—Wow I would kill to live there. <u>I'm stuck here in boring old England</u>.

DianaKleary: You are all cracking me up. <u>I'm in Bamberg, Germany. My dad is in the military</u>.

Tennispro444: Germany, wow. Its so neat we are all from different places. So where are you, Busybee?

Busybee: I don't know if I should tell you. POS! Hint—Big Apple.

DianaKleary: Oh come on, its not like it matters if we share where we are from. I mean what are the chances we'll ever meet?

Darthvader12: Ha Ha—you better give me your email address too Diana—you'll be talking to me again—remember you're going to help me with my math.

DianaKleary: OK, POS gone! DK@myisp.com—so simple.

Tennispro444: I'll email you too—I can do math and all but I think it would be cool to have pen pals. My parents want to take a trip to Europe and maybe I could convince them to see Germany.

DianaKleary: Oh sure, I can show you all the sights.

Busybee: Hey now I feel left out. You all can email me too—busybee@hotmessages. com. Oh, and you should all check out my MySpace page. I'm only 13, so I had to lie to get one. But its so cool. All of my friends are on there and you can see my pic and all. You can meet my list of friends too.

Darthvader12: Wow—I'll take a look. I want a MySpace page but my mom said absolutely not, I'm too young.

SmithinToronto: Well, I should get back to homework. Chat with you all again soon—same place tomorrow.

Online Extension

Managing your personal information online is about making sure you are creating the right digital impression. Information you post online on social sites, on chats or messaging programs, on forums, and on blogs stays around for a long time—even when you want to just forget about it. The information others can find about you online is called your "digital footprint." It is good to remember that a digital footprint can also include photos; *it is made up of anything posted by you or posted about you by others.* Obviously, it's important to check your digital footprint once in a while to see what others can find out about you. Think about it; it may not just be your friends who see this information, it can be anyone: your parents, your teachers, or anyone with Internet access!

One way to determine what is in your digital footprint is by googling your name (**Note:** Any search engine can be used) with quotation marks. For example, "first name last name." The results will show any public postings of your first and last name.

Younger or less experienced users will have smaller "footprints" compared to users who post more. Googling your own name may or may not turn up much information. This depends on your own posting history. A small footprint can be GREAT! Keep in mind that some employers and colleges look at an applicant's footprint.

Other people may have a larger footprint, such as your school principal, church pastor, or local politician. Follow your teacher's directions for googling different names.

Think about what you find about yourself and others. Is the information always good or positive? Is it always true?

Teacher: Make sure you preview any search names to ensure respectable search results are returned.

Put It Together

Answers will be subjective. Rules/tips created should include:
- Ask a parent before filling out an online profile or form.
- Do not fill out personal information unless absolutely necessary to do an activity.
- Enable privacy settings.
- Never send personal information in an e-mail.

Use What U Have Learned Answer Key

Name at least one way a student younger than thirteen can use online profiles or fill out online forms in a safe and appropriate way. **(Always ask an adult for advice and/or help when filling out any personal information online.)**

What advice would you give a child younger than you on how to be safe online when asked for personal information on a Web site or from a person only known from the Internet? (Always ask an adult for advice and/or help. Do not respond to requests for personal information.)

List instances in which you think your parents or other adults you know would probably need to provide personal information online for a good purpose. (Possible answers: when making online purchases, when signing up for a service, when paying bills, etc.)

What advice would you give an adult in regard to posting personal information online? (Possible answers: Enable privacy settings. Do not store credit card or address information online. Any tips given in the lessons.)

List instances in which you will probably need to provide personal information online for a good purpose. (When signing up for services or games. When submitting application forms for school or other physical-world activities, etc.)

Name at least one thing you will do to make sure you use online profiles or fill out online forms in a safe and appropriate way. (Answers will be subjective and should reflect safety concepts presented.)

Chat Wise

You may want to do this activity in a group setting and have students discuss and create appropriate answers for richNfamous.

4.3. Beyond Revealing Simple Information (page 119)

Sharing Picture Activity Answer Key

Ways a picture can be shared via digital technologies (examples: Web site viewing; download from Web site; e-mail attachment; instant message attachment; take picture with a cell phone and upload to Internet site; cell phone text attachment; webcam).

Kinds of personal information a photograph of you could tell another person (examples: How you look; physical characteristics, hair color, eye color, etc.; approximate age; hobbies, sports, interests; approximate location).

Use What U Have Learned Answer Key

Examples of do's and don'ts follow:

Do	Don't
Use an anonymous e-mail address if possible like: anonymous@tampabay.rr.com.	Use your real name in your e-mail address, like kristikeip@tampabay.rr.com.
Use a nickname in postings.	Use your real name in postings.
Keep postings fairly anonymous and non-identifying in content.	Post personal information that can lead to your whereabouts.
Post pictures ONLY if you have taken safety precautions such as Web site password protection.	Post pictures in public online areas.
Blog only if in a password-protected area.	Blog about personal life in public online areas.
Keep webcam use to phone calls and interactions with family and personal friends from the "real" world.	Use a webcam or post streaming video of your personal life in public online areas.
If someone really knows you he or she will know your IM screen name. Anyone who asks for it online could be dangerous.	Post your IM name in public online areas.

4.4. Truths About Online Strangers (page 122)

Terms to Know Definitions

- **acronym**—an identifier or code word formed from some of the letters (often the initials) of a phrase and used as an abbreviation; a word formed from the initial letters or groups of letters of words in a set phrase or series of words.
- **grooming process**—the process used by a predator to get a victim ready so the predator can easily do harm to the victim.
- **online predator**—one who stalks or uses lies and secrecy with Internet technologies to get close enough to another person in order to easily hurt or harm him or her.
- **prey**—a victim or one who is vulnerable to victimization by a predator.

Think About It—Talk About It Answer Key

Some common advice/rules about communicating with (talking to) strangers in the physical world.

Sample answers:

- Don't talk to strangers.
- Don't give personal information to strangers.
- Don't tell a stranger your address over the phone.

What R U Saying?

Text Messaging Savvy Answer Key

- The advantages of using acronyms in text messaging (quicker, less typing, easier to use with cell phones, be able to use this universal "language" like everyone else, write in code).
- How do you think the ease of text or instant messaging can help a stranger get information about another person (easy to be familiar/seem like you know someone, easy to get bits of information to put all together, easy to send and receive pictures)?

Put It Together Answer Key

The rule should reflect similar strategies that one would use regarding talking to strangers in the physical world.

Cyber Tales—Reflect Answer Key

1. She never gave out her phone number or address to any strange guys.
2. School name, team uniforms, practice times.

3. Subjective answer.

4. Immediately call for an adult's help; refuse to engage in conversation.

Use What U Have Learned Answer Key

Cause-and-effect scenarios. (Answers will be subjective but must reflect unsafe consequences to each cause.)

Use What U Have Learned Answer Key

Answers should reflect online privacy concepts and skills learned in these lessons.

4.5. Enrichment Activity—Wrap It Up (page 130)

Students provided with instructions on how to create an awareness campaign with Internet safety posters. *Note:* Enable this activity by preparing in advance a place for students to display their work.

Post-Assessment Reminder

- If you will end the i-SAFE program with this unit, have students complete the post-assessments online at http://www.isafe.org/activitybook.
- Students complete the Outcomes assessment three to six weeks after completion of the last i-SAFE lesson implemented.

4.6. Unit Review (page 132)

Instruct students when to complete the unit review.

Answer Key

1. c	6. true
2. d	7. false
3. c, d	8. false
4. a	9. false
5. d	10. false

Unit 4: Managing Personal Information Online (5–8) Student Pages

It is impossible to think of life in today's world without the Internet. Cyberspace offers instant communication and seemingly infinite resources for all no matter the age, location, occupation, or interests a person might have. In fact, using the Internet is no longer an isolated factor that helps us with tasks; it is a complete society in which real people engage in everyday life. It is important to realize that one's online actions today can have a real impact on one's online presence in the future.

Understanding the Activities

These activities are designed to help you understand and master a selection of basic online life skills dealing with the topic of sharing personal information online. Sections include:

4.1. Safeguarding Your Online Identity: Screen Names and Passwords

4. 2. Get Real About Online Profiles

4. 3. Beyond Revealing Simple Information

4. 4. Truths About Online Strangers

4. 5. Enrichment Activity—Wrap It Up!

4. 6. Unit Review

In addition to written activities, lesson sections include:

- **Learning Objectives:** Lists of the expected outcomes of what you are to understand upon completion of the lesson. Use the learning objectives to get a preview of lesson content before the lesson and as a guide to what you will be expected to know on the unit quiz.

- **Terms to Know:** Learn and practice critical terms and definitions associated with the lesson topic.

- **Think About It—Talk About It:** Thought-provoking questions to consider that, depending on classroom setup, can be directed to think about independently or discuss at home, with a partner, in a small group, or as a class.

- **Cyber Know-How:** Resource and/or skill-based information.

• **Cyber Tales:** Stories of real experiences on the "Net."

 • **Free Write:** Exploration of the topics through a writing prompt and space to jot down thoughts and previous knowledge.

 • **Use What U Have Learned:** Directed activity to support and/or demonstrate learning.

 • **Online Extension:** Activities set up by the instructor to go online and apply what has been learned, by either researching a topic or completing a task.

 • **Reaching Others:** Guidance for extending what has been learned by sharing information with others.

Additional Resources

Your instructor may provide you with additional online and/or offline resources to complete these activities.

4.1. Safeguarding Your Online Identity: Screen Names and Passwords

Learning Objectives

Upon completion of this section you should be able to:

- Assess the dangers in choosing an unsafe user name
- Classify the types of personal information that should be avoided in constructing a safe user name
- Assess the dangers in choosing an unsafe password
- Identify a strategy for making safe passwords
- Demonstrate how to create a secure password

Terms to Know

Define the following words. Underline and then use a dictionary to look up any words you don't know or are not sure of.

- anonymous _____
- appropriate _____
- identify _____
- inappropriate _____
- non-identifying _____
- online profile _____
- password _____
- personal information _____
- random _____
- screen name _____
- user ID _____

Think About It—Talk About It

The Internet is not anonymous. When you sign on, others have access to you. Your e-mail address, screen name, and password serve as barriers between you and others. You need to maintain this barrier by not giving out private information. There are many out there who would like to know more about you for a variety of reasons including:

- They could want to harm you.
- They could want to steal from you.
- They could use information to conduct their own business either by selling your information or by using it in an illegal manner.

Cyber Know-How

Screen names and user IDs represent you in Cyberspace. When you choose a screen name, you want something that allows you to remain anonymous or unknown to anyone you don't want your identity revealed to.

- In order to protect your identity in the physical world, online screen/user names should never include personal or identifying information, including (but not limited to):
    - Your real first and last name
    - Any part of your address
    - Your location (i.e., Chicagogirl, HaverhillGuy)
    - Your telephone number
    - Your e-mail address
- Do not use an inappropriate or suggestive name or word to describe yourself (i.e., sexyman42, hotbabygirl). You may attract the wrong kind of people.
- Do not use pornographic or obscene words.
- Be careful that you don't COMBINE pieces of personal information with other information that can be used to identify you or your location, such as in the screen name TSmith2012grad.

 **Use What U Have Learned**

Part 1

Look at the following screen names. Make a list of those that contain identifying (or potentially identifying) information and list the information that is (or may be) revealed.

GTaylorplaysGuitar   carrie_lewis@gmc.net   REMforever
Wellesleygirl   rockhound92008   Miamisue13
Canarielover   nymets2   brandonclassof2012
namelessjester5   andersonMJ   GerbilsRkewl

Part 2

List the screen names from above that do not contain identifying (non-identifying) information here:

Online ID: What Can You Tell?

Look at the screen names below. Jot down what each says about the person who chose it. Then, put the names in order from least informative (1) to most informative (5).

Screen Name	Information Revealed
Jessica4dance	
JSmthstealshome	
Bayareababe	
Dancinfun	
Fred14	

List a screen name that you have seen or know about that provides personal information, and describe why it is unsafe.

Think About It—Talk About It

What does your screen name say about you?

Your screen name may already be safe. If so, relate what you learn here to others you know—friends, brothers or sisters, even your parents! What do their screen names say about them?

Cyber Know-How: Password Security

A password is a series of letters, numbers, and/or symbols used to log you in to a computer system. Passwords are used to access e-mail, edit webpages, join chat rooms, etc. They are usually between six and eight characters long.

A password is of no use to you if it is not a complete secret.

- Don't tell anyone your password.
- Don't write your password down anywhere anyone can easily find it.
- When you decide on a password, make sure it cannot be guessed.
- If you think there's even a chance someone else might know your password, change it.
- Make sure no one is standing near you when you enter your password to gain access to an online source.

How to Create a Safe Password

A good password should . . .

- Be lengthy: at least eight characters
- Contain a combination of letters, numbers, and symbols
- Be changed when its secrecy is in doubt
- Not contain personal information
- Not be shared
- Not be easily guessed
- Not be provided in an e-mail, even if requested

What do you think? Is it safe to reveal one's interest or hobby in a password? Why or why not?

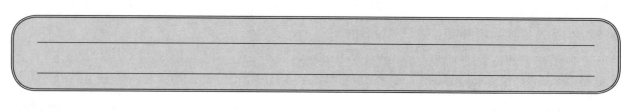

 ## Use What U Have Learned

The best passwords are made up of completely random letters, numbers, and symbols. However, there are tricks to making a password that can be remembered. One way is to take the first letters from a simple poem to create a password. For example:

"Three blind mice. See how they run." Could be used to create the password: **3bmShtr**

Create a rule for creating a safe password. *Hint:* Think of a way you might teach a younger person how to make a safe password. Then apply your rule by creating a sample password.

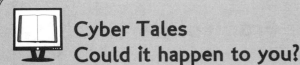

Cyber Tales
Could it happen to you?

Jared was angry with his friend Paul. They both had personal pages on a social networking site, and because they had been close friends, Paul had shared his user ID and account password with Jared. As a matter of fact, Jared knew that Paul used the same user ID and password for almost all of his online accounts. Feeling angry and frustrated, Jared accessed Paul's webpage and, once in, provided personal information and posted embarrassing pictures and comments about Paul on the site.

Free Write

Think about a password that you use online. Is it something obvious? Could someone easily guess it? If someone knows your password, he or she could pretend to be you. What kinds of dangers are involved when others know or guess your password?

Reaching Others

Often the ones who know the least about creating a safe password are adults. Parents often use the birth date of a child, their own Social Security number, or a pet's name as a password. Adults with families who use the Internet are especially at risk for online identity and monetary theft. They did not have the opportunity to learn about computer security when they were young. Share what you know with a family member today!

4.2. Get Real About Online Profiles

Learning Objectives

Upon completion of this section you should be able to:

- Understand that online strangers may want your personal information
- Recognize how to respond appropriately with personal information to Internet strangers
- Understand the risks of providing too much personal information in online profiles and forms

Terms to Know

- Appropriate
- Enable
- Online profile
- Privacy settings

Think About It—Talk About It

The "FBI Internet Safety Tips"

No doubt you have seen or heard lots of Internet safety tips. These tips are important because they (1) create "awareness" about problems people can run into on the Internet and (2) usually provide an easy "tip" to avoid danger. Read through the following Internet safety tips developed by the Federal Bureau of Investigation (FBI) for children in grades K through 5.

- First, remember never to give out personal information such as your name, home address, school name, or telephone number in a chat room or on bulletin boards. Also, never send a picture of yourself to someone you chat with on the computer without your parents' permission.
- Never write to someone who has made you feel uncomfortable or scared.
- Do not meet someone or have the person visit you without the permission of your parents.

- Tell your parents right away if you read anything on the Internet that makes you feel uncomfortable.
- Remember that people online may not be who they say they are. Someone who says that "she" is a "twelve-year-old girl" could really be an older man.

Online Profiles

Your online profile provides the information that you submit to describe yourself either in a form or in communication. A common Internet safety tip is to "Never give out personal information online."

As a matter of fact, it is against the law for Web sites to ask for personal, identifying information from anyone thirteen years old or younger.

 Activity

Fill out the sample online profile below truthfully.

MY PROFILE

Name:

Street address:

City:

Country:

Phone number:

E-mail address:

Date of birth:

Gender:

Number of people in your family:

School name:

Favorite celebrity:

Favorite music:

Favorite sport:

Use your profile to answer the following questions:

- Would you be comfortable handing that form out to strangers on the street? Why or why not?

  _____

  _____

- Would your parents want you to hand that form out to strangers on the street? Why or why not?

  _____

  _____

- Would you feel comfortable handing that form to a known criminal? Why or why not?

  _____

  _____

- When you fill out a profile online, can/do you determine who will look at it?

  _____

  _____

 ## Cyber Know-How

Most online profiles ask for much more information than is required. Required information is usually indicated by an asterisk (*) or the word "required." If you must complete an online profile, it is safest to fill in required information only.

 ## Think About It—Talk About It

- Does any of your personal/identifying information already exist in online profiles?
- Are all of your online profiles necessary for the activities you normally do online, or can one or more be deleted?

 ## Cyber Know-How—Privacy Settings

If you have not enabled privacy settings (some profiles do not provide privacy settings), the personal information you give out in an online profile can be searched by strangers.

When in doubt:

- Think twice before replying online or giving out personal information.
- Don't be afraid to ask for parental or adult guidance when filling out information online. They might learn something too!

Go Online

- Access your existing online profiles and check to see the kinds of information you have provided that can be searched by other users.
- Enable privacy settings where possible.
- Revise profiles that say too much about you.

Reality Check

It is unrealistic to think that we will not give up personal information online. Sometimes we all DO need to post some personal information in online profiles and on forms to be able to use the Internet for good purposes. The trick is to know when, where, and how much to reveal.

Everything you say about yourself builds a "profile" of you for others to see. It pays to be aware ahead of time of where you will probably be asked for personal information on the Web. This allows you to establish guidelines for yourself about when you will provide the information safely and when you should get a second opinion from a trusted adult.

Watch out for online communication dangers . . . . . . on Web sites

- **Pop-ups.** You are a WINNER! Surfing the Web often provides lots of pop-ups offering free merchandise, contests, and survey forms to fill out. Information you provide can be used to create e-mail spam and will make MORE pop-ups!
- **Web sites you visit.** Some Web sites ask you for private information before you can access their stuff. Make sure you ask your parents before giving anyone private information on online forms.
- **On your own Web site.** Many young people now have their own Web sites or social networking pages. Be cautious about what information you display.

List some things you have seen on webpages that are not very safe.

_____   _____
_____   _____
_____   _____
_____   _____
_____   _____
_____   _____
_____   _____
_____   _____
_____   _____
_____   _____

 ## Cyber Tales

In 2005 a student was suspended from school for posting "harsh" comments about a teacher on an online blog. The teacher was not named, but the name of the student who made the comments was identifiable.

A 2007 article told about a high school student who used his personal Web site to blog: "Kill Alaina!" about an irritating friend. The posting was made on a personal computer while in the privacy of his home, but the Web site was not password protected. One month later he found himself in the dean's office facing disciplinary action at school. His parents were brought in for a conference and it was discovered at that time that the student lived out of the correct zone for the school he was attending. The final result was that the student had to change schools. It is interesting to note that, after the fact, a photo of the student was circulated along with an article about the story.

Do U blog? Unless it's on your own password-protected site, you have no control over what happens to blog postings or other text posted on Web sites.

112   Unit 4: Managing Personal Information Online (5–8)

Watch out for online communication dangers . . .
. . . in e-mail

- **Spam.** Many companies advertise via e-mail and ask for more information about you. Do not respond to these e-mails—DELETE them!
- **Be careful when you reply to an e-mail.** You are including your e-mail address and you don't know where it will go from there.
- **Remember that the sender of an e-mail may not be someone you know.** Don't send personal information, photographs, etc.

. . . when chatting, IMing, or gaming
Instant communication can result in revealing information you wouldn't normally reveal. This can leave you open to harm.

- **Keep online interaction online.** Don't agree to meet or phone people met online.
- **Don't give out identifying information** publicly when online.
- **Private chats aren't always private.** When you meet offline friends online in a private chat room, be careful. Others can often enter and lurk (watch what you are saying about yourself).

 **Online Extension**

Managing your personal information online is about making sure you are creating the right digital impression. Information you post online on social sites, on chats or messaging programs, on forums, and on blogs stays around for a long time—even when you want to just forget about it. The information others can find about you online is called your "digital footprint." It is good to remember that a digital footprint can also include photos; *it is made up of anything posted by you or posted about you by others.* Obviously, it's important to check your digital footprint once in a while to see what others can find out about you. Think about it; it may not just be your friends who see this information, it can be anyone: your parents, your teachers, or anyone with Internet access!

One way to determine what is in your digital footprint is by googling your name (***Note:*** any search engine can be used) with quotation marks. For example, "first name last name." The results will show any public postings of your first and last name.

Younger or less experienced users will have smaller "footprints" compared to users who post more. Googling your own name may or may not turn up much information. This depends on your own posting history. A small footprint can be GREAT! Keep in mind that some employers and colleges look at an applicant's footprint.

 ## Activity

Read the chat transcript below and circle the personal information that could lead to identification and location of the chatters.

i-SAFE	CHAT				▢ ▢ X
File	Edit	View	Favorite	Tools	Help

◀ ▶ ☒ ↻ ⌂

http://www.isafe.org [GO]

Darthvader12: Hey what's everyone up to?

Busybee: Not much here. I've been working on math homework.

DianaKleary: Math – that's my favorite subject! LOL!

Tennispro444: Are u nuts girl? Math! I'd rather get my teeth pulled than do math.

Darthvader12: So you're a math whiz Diana – maybe you could help me with my algebra.

DianaKleary: Sure no problem – Darthvader12 – what is your real name anyway?

Darthvader12: Bryan

DianaKleary: OK – now I know U☺- no problem. I tutor at my school – this is my cell. Ask me a ? anytime. 443-773-6691

Busybee: so darth ru like a huge Star Wars fan or something?

Darthvader12: yeah pretty much

SmithinToronto: That is neat. Me I'm not much into videos. I'd rather listen to music. KWIM?

Busybee: Hey Smith, ?4U - Are you in Toronto? Is it snowing there?

SmithinToronto: I live right across from Air Canada Centre. No snow yet. But its cold!

Tennispro444: I've never seen snow. We don't see much of it in Hawaii lol

Darthvader12: Hawaii – Wow I would kill to live there. I'm stuck here in boring old England.

DianaKleary: You are all cracking me up. I'm in Germany. My dad is in the military.

Tennispro444: Germany, wow. Its so neat we are all from different places. So where are you Busy bee?

Busybee: I don't know if I should tell you. POS! Hint - Big Apple.

DianaKleary: Oh come on, its not like it matters if we share where we are from. I mean what are the chances we'll ever meet.

Darthvader12: Ha Ha – you better give me your email address too Diana – you'll be talking to me again – remember you're going to help me with my math.

DianaKleary: Ok, POS gone! DK@myisp.com - so simple.

Tennispro444: I'll email you too – I can do math and all but I think it would be cool to have pen pals. My parents want to take a trip to Europe and maybe I could convince them to see Germany.

DianaKleary: Oh sure, I can show you all the sights.

Busybee: Hey now I feel left out. You all can email me too – busybee@hotmessages.com. Oh, and you should all check out my MySpace page. I'm only 13, so I had to lie to get one. But its so cool. All of my friends are on there and you can see my pic and all. You can meet my list of friends too.

Darthvader12: wow – I'll take a look. I want a myspace page but my mom said absolutely not I'm too young.

SmithinToronto: Well, I should get back to homework. Chat with you all again soon – same place tomorrow

CHAT:

Other people may have a larger footprint such as your school principal, church pastor, or local politician. Follow your teacher's directions for googling different names.

Think about what you find about yourself and others. Is the information always good or positive? Is it always true?

Put It Together

Think about the answers to the following questions:

- Where have you seen personal information asked for on the Internet?
- How do you know whether these requests for information are valid?

In the first column below make a list of examples of online instances in which a person might be asked to give up personal information unnecessarily.

In the second column create a list of safety rules/tips that can help one respond appropriately to online requests for personal information.

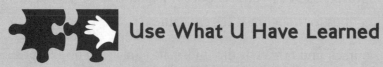

Use What U Have Learned

Name at least one way a student younger than thirteen can use online profiles or fill out online forms in a safe and appropriate way.

_____

_____

_____

What advice would you give a child younger than you on how to be safe online when asked for personal information on a Web site or from a person only known from the Internet?

_____

_____

_____

List instances in which you think your parents or other adults you know would probably need to provide personal information online for a good purpose.

_____

_____

_____

What advice would you give an adult in regard to posting personal information online?

_____

_____

List instances in which you will probably need to provide personal information online for a good purpose.

_____

_____

_____

Name at least one thing you will do to make sure you use online profiles or fill out online forms in a safe and appropriate way.

_____

_____

_____

Chat Wise

For the screen name, "richNfamous" write in chat responses to two other chatters, kewlio and frenz550, without revealing personal information in an unsafe way.

```
┌──────────────────────────────────────────────────────────────────────────┐
│ i-SAFE  |   CHAT                                              [_] [□] [x]   │
├──────────────────────────────────────────────────────────────────────────┤
│   File        Edit        View       Favorite      Tools       Help        │
├──────────────────────────────────────────────────────────────────────────┤
│  ◄  ►  ☒ ↻⌂                                                                 │
├──────────────────────────────────────────────────────────────────────────┤
│  http://www.isafe.org                                           [ GO ]     │
├──────────────────────────────────────────────────────────────────────────┤
```

frenz550: O GR8 Im loaded with homework!!!!!

kewlio: I sooo sympathize—my science project is due in a week.

richNfamous: Really—what school do you go to? I _____

frenz550: Diablo in Denver.

kewlio: My folks sent me to a military school, but its kewl we go just about anywhere on weekends. U like the beach? There's one near here.

frenz550: XLNT! I luv the beach! Send me pics. What about U richNfamous? What do U do for fun? Where do U live?

richNfamous: _____

kewlio: U haven't lived till you tried surfing. Send me your e-mails and I'll show you a neat pix of this 10 foot wave I caught one day.

frenz550: awesome—mine is frenz550@co.rr.com

richNfamous: _____

kewlio: I always wanted to visit Colorado—climb some mountains. U been there richNfamous?

richNfamous: _____

kewlio: Hey how old r u two anyway?

frenz550: 13—but almost 14

richNfamous: _____

kewlio: that's kewl. Gotta go now. CUL!

frenz550: me2. TNT richNfamous!

End of chat

```
┌──────────┬─────────────────────────────────────────────────────────────────┐
│  CHAT:   │                                                                   │
└──────────┴─────────────────────────────────────────────────────────────────┘
```

 **Use What U Have Learned**

Did you provide any personal information in the chat? Describe why you think it was, or was not, a risk to post this information.

_____

_____

_____

_____

_____

_____

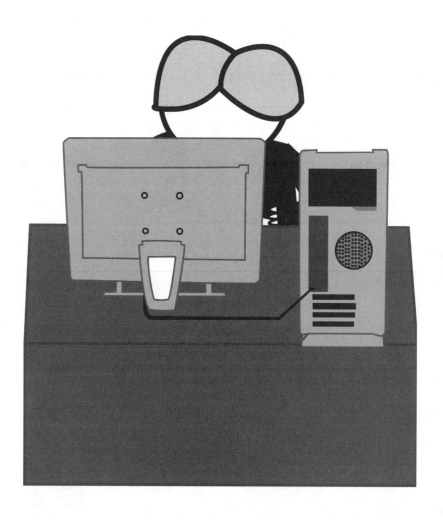

4.3. Beyond Revealing Simple Information

Learning Objectives

Upon completion of this section you should be able to:

- Understand a broader view of the impact of providing personal information online
- Identify other ways personal information is provided through digital technology
- Identify strategies to safeguard privacy using a variety of digital technologies

Terms to Know

"Permanence"—being able to exist for an indefinite duration

Have you ever thought about the permanence to the information you post online? Unlike a paper form or a picture that you can destroy, information posted online can take on a life of its own that you never intended. In other words, it can be very difficult to get rid of an online posting—even impossible.

Activity

Digital technology allows us to share personal information in many ways beyond chatting, blogging, and filling out online forms. Have you heard the phrase, "A picture is worth a thousand words?"

List ways a picture can be shared via digital technologies. (Yes! Include cell phones.)

Now list the kinds of personal information a photograph of you could tell another person.

Use What U Have Learned

Based on what you now know about keeping personal information private on the Internet, for every "DO" tip below, create a corresponding "DON'T" tip:

Do	Don't
Use an anonymous e-mail address if possible like: anonymous@tampabay.rr.com.	
Use a nickname in postings.	
Keep postings fairly anonymous and non-identifying in content.	
Post pictures ONLY if you have taken safety precautions such as Web site password protection.	
Blog only if in a password-protected area.	
Keep webcam use to phone calls and interactions with family and personal friends from the "real" world.	
If someone really knows you they will know your IM screen name. Anyone who asks for it online could be dangerous.	

 # Cyber Know-How—Global Positioning System (GPS)

Have you heard about GPS?

Many cars and cell phones include this technology to help us find our way around. GPS is a good thing, but providing your "global position" to a stranger could be very dangerous.

Fortunately, most of the time that is not as easy as it sounds. In general, you can not track someone using his or her cell phone, unless the person you want to track has the right kind of cell phone, connected to the right network, with the right service and software. And that means the person can't track you either.

However, if your cell phone has this capability (a GPS tracking application), you should know that tracking someone without his or her knowledge can get you in trouble. Typically, a cell phone user must first give permission to be tracked, and the phone must be enabled for tracking.

Be SAFE!

If GPS applies to technology you own, learn how to disable the tracking application to maintain safety. Use it only with permission from a parent.

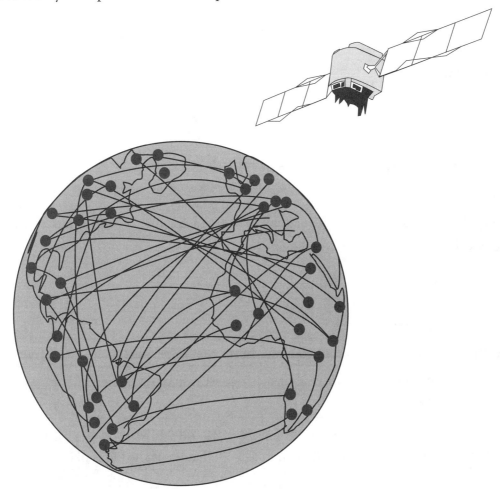

4.4. Truths About Online Strangers

Learning Objectives

Upon completion of this section you should be able to:

- Understand that an online stranger is anyone met exclusively online
- List safety rules/advice of behavior toward strangers in the physical community that also apply to behavior toward strangers in Cyberspace
- Recognize the basic steps in an online predator's grooming process
- Recognize how to respond appropriately/safely to Internet strangers

Terms to Know

- acronym
- grooming process
- online predator
- prey

Think About It—Talk About It

Think about what you like to do online. Chances are, at least one of the things you like to do online involves chatting or texting with others.

Answer either "yes" or "no" to the following questions:

1. Do you talk to "strangers" online?	**yes no**
2. Do you talk to anyone online whom you have never met in person?	**yes no**
3. Are there people online whom you chat or message with so often that you consider them to be your friends?	**yes no**
4. Can you really be sure that someone you know only from the Internet is telling the truth about him- or herself, such as age or what he or she looks like?	**yes no**

List some common advice/rules about communicating with (talking to) strangers in the physical world.

_____

_____

_____

_____

_____

What R U Saying?
Text Messaging Savvy

What are the advantages of using acronyms in text messaging? List at least three.

_____

_____

_____

How do you think the ease of text or instant messaging can help a stranger get information about another person?

_____

_____

_____

Put It Together

Your rules from the activity at the top of the page also apply online. Anyone known exclusively online (not a known friend from the physical community) is a stranger. Nothing is really known about this type of person.

Create a rule to maintain safety while texting:

_____

_____

_____

Predators and Prey
Let's define "online predator."

- Think about what the word "predator" means to you. Does the word make you think of lions hunting for their next meal?
- A predator is one who stalks or uses lies, secrecy, or stealth, to get close enough to another person in order to easily hurt or harm him or her.
- Now think about what the word "prey" means to you.
- "Prey" is one who is a victim or one who is vulnerable to victimization by a predator (the lion's meal!).

We also use these words in terms of the Internet:

Some people lie about who they are and what they want on the Internet for various reasons. Sometimes it is to steal an identity or to bully. Other times it is to meet children and teens to form an inappropriate relationship. These people are known as "online predators." The people who are the intended victims are the "prey."

Signs of a Predator

If you know what to look for and pay attention to how online strangers behave, it is fairly easy to spot someone who might be a predator. Predators use a process called "grooming"—grooming means they are getting the victim ready so they can easily do harm to them. We call this the grooming process:

1. The predator pretends to have the same interests, likes, and dislikes as the victim to create an online friendship.
2. The predator builds trust by listening to anything the victim wants to talk about.
3. The predator establishes secrecy by telling the victim that it is better that he or she do not tell anyone about their special friendship.
4. Then the predator tries to break down barriers by convincing the victim that there is nothing the two of them can't share. Sometimes the predator will use inappropriate language and send inappropriate pictures.
5. Sometimes a predator will threaten to tell the victim's parents or, even worse, hurt his or her family, if the victim tells about their friendship.
6. Face-to-face meetings are the goal of every predator—to meet the victim alone in the real world.

Online people are not always who they appear to be.

Think About It—Talk About It

Online friendships can be great! However, if anyone uses any of the steps of the grooming process on you or one of your friends, be suspicious! A person who behaves in any of these ways is not behaving appropriately on the Internet, and should not be considered to be any kind of friend unless he or she changes his or her ways.

Cyber Know-How—Minimizing Danger from Online Strangers

There are things you can do to minimize the danger and the chances of becoming prey to an online predator. These safety precautions include choosing a safe screen name, not revealing information on the Internet, and carefully choosing whom to communicate with.

No matter what, it is important to tell an adult if you ever feel uncomfortable online or are approached by someone who discusses inappropriate things or wants to meet you offline.

Cyber Tales

Most teenagers and young adults these days have been online. Certainly there are plenty of good reasons to use the Internet—hanging out with friends, doing research, and playing games. Unfortunately, there is increasing danger involved in getting too personal with people met online.

Take Brittany for example. Brittany was a young girl who liked to hang out, play tennis, and chat on the Internet, especially with tenniskid, a friend she met while online. Even though they had never met in person, she and tenniskid were instant friends. Brittany had described her school, all about how much she practices—when and where—and the new team uniforms in great detail. She was going to talk her parents into letting her go to the same tennis camp as tenniskid. There was an element of mystery about tenniskid because she told Brittany she wanted her to guess her real name. She said she liked to surprise people. Brittany had never had such a fun friend.

Continued

Brittany felt safe on the Internet. To her, it wasn't like she chatted with anyone she didn't know! Besides, she never gave out her home address or phone number to any strange guys. It had gotten so the only person she chatted with lately was tenniskid anyway, and she knew her! However, even without sharing her address, Brittany had supplied enough information in their conversations to be located offline. And more importantly, the two had built a trusting friendship, even though they had never met in person.

One afternoon Brittany noticed that an unfamiliar man watched her tennis practice after school. As she was leaving, he approached her and, with a big smile, said, "Brittany—I have a surprise for you. What do you think? It's me, tenniskid!"

Reflect

Apply information from the Internet safety tips and strategies you have learned in these lessons to Brittany's story and answer the following:

1. Name ways that Brittany showed she was aware of being safe with strangers online.

   _____

   _____

2. What information did Brittany give tenniskid that allowed her to be located?

   _____

   _____

3. How do you think Brittany felt when she learned the true identity of tenniskid?

   _____

   _____

4. Explain a way Brittany could respond safely to tenniskid's surprise?

   _____

   _____

 ## Use What U Have Learned

Complete the following cause-and-effect scenarios.

1. Janice reveals her name and age to an online chat buddy.

   - **Effect:** The online chat buddy turns out to be a predator who lures her to a meeting and tries to harm her.

- Other possible effects/consequences to her actions:

  _____

  _____

  _____

- How could the effects/consequences have been avoided?

  _____

  _____

  _____

2. Mark uses his e-mail address as a screen name for a bulletin board.
   - **Effect:** His e-mail box is flooded with spam, retail announcements, etc.
   - Other possible effects/consequences:

     _____

     _____

     _____

   - How could the effects/consequences have been avoided?

     _____

     _____

     _____

3. Sarah is a big fan of her local football team—the Dallas Cowboys. Everyone at school knows this. Her password is Cowboygirl.
   - **Effect:** Sarah's ex-boyfriend has an idea of what her password is, guesses it, and uses her account to send bad e-mail to others. Now everyone is mad at her.
   - Other possible effects/consequences:

     _____

     _____

     _____

   - How could the effects/consequences have been avoided?

     _____

     _____

     _____

Continued

4. Mary's screen name is hotchick15. She uses it whenever she's chatting.

- **Effect:** Mary receives lots of harassment on the chat sites.
- Other possible effects/consequences:

_____

_____

_____

- How could the effects/consequences have been avoided?

_____

_____

_____

5. Eric has chosen a screen name that reflects allegiance to a gang.

- **Effect:** He recently received more than fifty hate mail messages and threats.
- Other possible effects/consequences:

_____

_____

_____

- How could the effects/consequences have been avoided?

_____

_____

_____

6. When Andy signed up for an instant messaging service, he filled out his personal profile with all his information and did not enable the privacy settings.

- **Effect:** Everyone on the Internet can find out who he is and what he posted. They can use this information in any way.
- Other possible effects/consequences:

_____

_____

_____

- How could the effects/consequences have been avoided?

_____

_____

_____

7. Chad has been e-mailing a girl he met online. She asks him to send a picture. He does.

- **Effect:** Chad was browsing the Web and finds his picture, but it's been changed so that he looks like he weighs five hundred pounds.

- Other possible effects/consequences:

_____

_____

_____

- How could the effects/consequences have been avoided?

_____

_____

_____

Best Advice

Online friendships can be fun, but always consider what kind of information you are sharing.

If you notice that one of your online friendships is following the grooming process pattern, proceed very cautiously. There is no reason for an online friend to want to have a secret relationship with you and/or to force you to meet in person without anyone else knowing about it.

Let your friends and family know about people you meet online and tell someone immediately if you are threatened or feel uncomfortable about anything that is said or sent online.

 ## Use What U Have Learned

Your friend keeps telling you about her online friend. Lately the online friend has been sending e-mails asking to meet at the movies alone. Put into your own words how you would tell your friend how to handle this situation safely.

_____

_____

_____

_____

4.5. Enrichment Activity—Wrap It Up!

Use the information on this page as a guideline to help others learn about managing their online identities.

Draw Attention with Internet Safety Posters
Create Awareness Art That Promotes Internet Safety!

One of the best ways to reach out and get your message across is through expression. A creative poster that inspires, educates, and motivates students to be responsible and safe online is right at your fingertips.

Gather Materials!

- Cardboard, poster board, or butcher paper—anything easy to paint or write on
- Paint and paint brushes
- Crayons, markers, pencils
- Masking tape (to attach posters to windows or doors)
- Magazines
- Scissors
- Glue
- **Optional:** Computer software (such as Adobe Photoshop, Illustrator, Microsoft Paint) to enhance or create your awareness art digitally

Build It!

Draw a rough idea of what you'd like the poster to look like below.

Internet Safety is the theme. Remember to use powerful words and bold pictures to catch everyone's attention. You can use quotes, song lyrics, or passages from a book. (Be sure to cite your source.) You can even cut out lettering or photos from old magazines to use. Next, get to work! Take your idea and make it come to life.

Post It!

Put your poster up where the most people will see it. A poster is only as good as its location. Be sure to ask your principal before you hang posters around school. If your class is creating a large number of posters, create a cyber art gallery in the school library, cafeteria, or main hallway. Create a "Hallway of Inspiration" motivating students to be safe online. You can also ask your favorite restaurant or store whether you can hang a poster in the window to get the message out to the community!

Be creative! A poster that draws attention is one that gets your message across!

Let i-SAFE Know!

Take a picture of your poster(s) and e-mail to **education@isafe.org**. Your art may be featured in future i-SAFE materials.

4.6. Unit Review

1. The best way to protect your personal Web site is to:

   a. Not reveal your name

   b. Not post pictures

   c. Password protect it

   d. Blog only about your friends

2. A password should be:

   a. Easily remembered

   b. A common word

   c. Your birth date or other info

   d. A random pairing of characters

3. People need information about online profile safety because (choose all that are true):

   a. They forget that they must never fill out an online profile.

   b. Posting an online profile is required to enter every Web site.

   c. Chances are good that they will need to fill out an online profile to use an Internet service.

   d. Online profiles can be searched by strangers.

4. Which of the following screen names is the safest?

   a. richnfamous

   b. johnsmith

   c. joe94

   d. richnfamous14

5. It _____ safe to post a photo of yourself online.

   a. is always

   b. is never

   c. is rarely

   d. can be

6. It's not a good idea to keep your online password(s) written down somewhere close to the computer. True or false?

   a. true

   b. false

7. Reveal your online password(s) to no more than one person. True or false?

    a. true

    b. false

8. It is never safe to use a webcam. True or false?

    a. true

    b. false

9. Adults do not need to worry about keeping their personal information private on the Internet. True or False?

    a. true

    b. false

10. Your e-mail address is a good choice for your screen name if it contains random characters. True of False?

    a. true

    b. false

Unit 5: A Common-Sense Approach to Strangers Online (5–8)

Unit Goal

Throughout the lesson/activities, learners will develop an understanding of the need to make responsible choices to ensure personal safety.

Understanding the Unit Format

This guide will provide you with discussion guidance, answers to activities, and explanations of the content of the student pages.

A Common-Sense Approach to Strangers Online lesson/activity sections include:

5.1. Online Identity Basics

5.2. Online Strangers, Predators, and the Grooming Process

5.3. Willing Participation

5.4. The Future of the Internet and YOU

5.5. Enrichment Activity—Wrap It Up!

5.6. Unit Review

Additional Resources

Refer to the i-SAFE *i-EDUCATOR Times* newsletters located at www.isafe.org and general i-SAFE lesson plans on similar topics for additional resource materials and background information if needed.

Prepare for the Lesson
Pre-Assessment

- If beginning the i-SAFE program with this unit, administer the pre-assessment online at http://www.isafe.org/activitybook.
- Enter School ID# 24615.

Post-Assessment

- If you will end the i-SAFE program with this unit, have students complete the post-assessment online at http://www.isafe.org/activitybook.
- Students complete the Outcomes assessment three to six weeks after completion of the last i-SAFE lesson implemented.

Plan Your Format

This unit is designed to enable transition from traditional class lessons to a more self-guided format, depending on student reading abilities.

1. Arrange for students to take the online pre-assessment.
2. Review the student activity pages and determine how you will implement the unit.
3. *Optional:* Prepare any additional reference material of your choice, including Internet access.
4. Provide each student with a copy of the student pages and review directions for student use.

Implementation Options

The following are suggested options for implementing the unit.

Group guided: Use the activities as short lessons over a period of time (one or two weeks to complete). This option is especially recommended for students with less developed reading comprehension skills.

- Have students complete the online pre-assessment prior to engaging in the i-SAFE program.
- Assign and go over each activity page with the class as a large group and have students complete them as instructed. You may want to have students read over text parts together to reinforce meaning.
- Go over completed pages with the group as they are finished.
- Have students complete the online post-assessment.
- Complete the empowerment activity suggested, or create your own activity.

Small groups: Students work in groups to complete the activities. This may be done in several sessions.

- Have students complete the online pre-assessment prior to engaging in the i-SAFE program.
- Introduce the unit with the pre-activity discussion.
- Create small work groups of three to four students.
- Student groups complete the assigned pages for each session and discuss their answers within the group.
- Go over the Wrap-Up activity to review the concepts presented in the unit.
- Have students complete the online post-assessment.
- Complete the empowerment activity suggested, or create your own activity.

Semi-self-guided: This option should only be considered for age-proficient readers. Create a timeline for activities to be completed.

- Have students complete the online pre-assessment prior to engaging in the i-SAFE program.
- Introduce the unit with the Activity 1 discussion.
- Have students complete their assignments.
- Go over the Wrap-Up activity to review the concepts.
- Have students complete the online post-assessment.
- Complete the empowerment activity suggested, or create your own activity.

5.1. Online Identity Basics (page 148)

Introduce the Unit

- Have a student read aloud the introduction at the top of page 144 to introduce the unit.
- As a class, go over the explanations of the sections in "Understanding the Activities."
- Have students complete the activities according to the implementation format you have chosen.

Terms to Know Answer Key

Terms in bold are the answers to the fill-in-the-blanks.

1. Online posting of one's characteristics or qualities make up his or her online **profile**.
2. **User ID** and **screen name** both mean online nickname or identity.
3. If an online identity is unsuitable or improper, we say that it is **inappropriate**.
4. Many people think they are completely **anonymous** while online, but unfortunately just being connected to the Internet provides identifying information about the user.
5. **Personal information** describes a person's identity such as name, date of birth, address, etc.
6. It is **appropriate** for people to use the Internet for education, recreation, and socializing if done safely.
7. The use of **non-identifying** terms for screen names and user IDs is one way to maintain a safe profile online.
8. It may signal danger if someone tries to obtain personal information from another in an **indirect** way.

Use What U Have Learned Answer Key

Students create an appropriate screen name for each of the people described. Answers can be any random selections of words, letters, numbers, etc., as long as they DO NOT contain identifying information included in each person's description.

Jackson's Profile

Name: Jackson Anderson

Age: 15

Sex: Male

Location: San Diego, California

Schools: San Diego High School
2006-2009

Music: Just sounds produced by vocals, guitars, basses, and drums...

Television: The Simpsons, South Park, MTV

Movies: Transformers, Blades of Glory, Stars Wars

Books: Redwulf's Curse, The Cry of Icemark

Heroes: My Mom

Groups: Soccer Team, Boys and Girls Club

Status: Single

Orientation: Straight

Hometown: San Diego

Body Type: 4" 6'

Zodiac Sign: Pisces

Smoke/Drink: No/No

Children: Undecided

Education: High School

Religion: Christian

Here for: Networking, Friends

Ethnicity: Caucasian

Think Out of the Box Answer Key

Answers will vary. Students create a safer profile for the person in the previous activity.

Think About It

Class discussion opportunity; discuss the following:

- Does any of your personal/identifying information already exist in online profiles?
- Are all of your online profiles necessary for the activities you normally do online, or can one or more be deleted?
- How much information about yourself have you made public in online conversations?

Online and Out of Control Answer Key

Students brainstorm a list of things that might happen to personal information as soon as it is placed online. Examples include:

- Identity can be stolen.
- The information can be saved by others for future use.
- Location can be identified.
- Picture can be altered and/or sent to others via e-mail or posted on a Web site without permission.

Activity—Sample Chat

Sample answers and review are provided in the student materials on page 152.

5.2. Online Strangers, Predators, and the Grooming Process (page 159)

Cyber Tale Answer Key

1. Answers will be subjective. Examples:
   - He paid special attention to her.
   - He gave her a gift (bus ticket).
2. Answers will be subjective. Examples:
   - She considered him to be a special friend.
   - She was caught up in the excitement of the friendship/relationship.
3. Answers will be subjective. Examples:
   - He recognized her technology knowledge and ability.
   - She enjoyed the secrecy of the situation.
   - She was convinced that it was right to keep what she was doing a secret from her parents.
4. Answers will be subjective. Examples:
   - She was lonely.
   - She enjoyed the attention and excitement.

Think About It—Talk About It

Discussion opportunity.

According to law enforcement experts, predators almost always pose as teenagers at first, using fake pictures and phony online profiles. Once they've gained the victim's trust, they slowly reveal their true age.

Would you know whether someone else's profile was a fake?

Continue the discussion with the next section.

What Do You Think?

Fact or Fiction. Cyber predators are only a problem for girls. Read the scenario and discuss.

Put It Together Answer Key

Answers should be similar to the following:

1. Established similar interests through chats: "Kelly met a person in a chat room who had the same interests in life that she did."

2. Built trust: Chatted for a month and then decided to meet.

3. Kept it a secret: (1) "He had convinced Kelly that it would be a lot easier to keep things a secret from friends and family—just too many questions to have to answer!" (2) "He gave her instructions on how to remove the hard drive from her computer."

4. Broke down barriers: We do not know whether inappropriate material was sent to Kelly, but he did make everything seem easy so that she did not have to worry about the details of meeting—sent taxi and bus ticket.

5. We do not know whether this predator made threats.

6. Meet face-to-face: sent taxi and bus ticket and met her at the bus.

Use What U Have Learned Answer Key

Answers will be subjective and should reflect safety strategies.

5.3. Willing Participation (page 165)

Think About It—Talk About It

Facilitate a discussion based the questions in this section.

Put It Together Answer Key

1. What are some safety/security risks Christina took when online?
   - Talked to a stranger about personal things.
   - Screen name was Long 2 hot 4 u.
   - Kept information about her chatting a secret from her aunt.

2. What part did Christina's screen name play in the development of her relationship with Saul?
   - It was provocative.
   - Brought sexual attention to her.

3. What part did Saul's screen name play in the development of her relationship with Christina?
   - Demonstrated interest in one of Christina's favorite interests.

4. List possible reasons why Christina considered Saul to be a trustworthy friend.
   - He paid a lot of attention to her.
   - He made her feel comfortable.
   - He listened to her.

5. List ways that Saul "groomed" Christina to be his victim.
   - Established similar interests: fast cars.
   - Built trust by listening to everything she had to say and showed that he cared.
   - Encouraged Christina to keep the relationship a secret from her aunt.
   - Talked on the phone—made her feel comfortable enough to make a date.
   - Ended in a face-to-face meeting.

6. Why do we call Christina a willing participant in the relationship?
   - She wanted to have this friendship.
   - She kept it a secret.
   - She was anxious to meet him.

Your Turn Answer Key

Responses will be subjective.

Create a List of Safety Tips

Evaluate safety tips by age appropriateness: young children should seek the help of an adult when communicating online. Tips should include safeguarding personal information from strangers.

5.4. The Future of the Internet and YOU (page 170)
Free Write—You Are Shaping Cyberspace!

Answers will be subjective.

Online Extension

You have just written a short essay on youth behaviors, current freedoms, online laws, and more. Take the time now to share that essay with i-SAFE. You can submit your writing (300-word maximum) through e-mail to activitybook@isafe.org. i-SAFE will use these essays to spot behavioral trends, shape lessons, advocate for legislation, publish, use in teaching examples, and more. Writers will be anonymous if their works are chosen but are playing an important role and part in improving the future of the Internet. Share your writing with us now!

5.5. Enrichment Activity—Wrap It Up! (page 173)

Students are provided with instructions on how to create and distribute an informative brochure or flyer to help others who may be at risk of being a victim of an Internet predator. Help with copying and distributing the finished brochures.

Post-Assessment Reminder

- If you will end the i-SAFE program with this unit, have students complete the post-assessments online at http://www.isafe.org/activitybook.
- Students complete the Outcomes assessment three to six weeks after completion of the last i-SAFE lesson implemented.

5.6. Unit Review (page 175)

Instruct students when to complete the unit review.

Answer Key

1. c
2. d
3. a, b, c
4. a
5. b
6. d
7. a—true
8. b—false
9. b—false
10. b—false

It is impossible to think of life in today's world without the Internet. Cyberspace offers instant communication and seemingly infinite resources for all no matter the age, location, occupation, or interests a person might have. In fact, using the Internet is no longer an isolated factor that helps us with tasks; it is a complete society in which real people engage in everyday life. It is important to realize that one's online actions today can have a real impact on one's online presence in the future.

Understanding the Activities

These activities are designed to help you understand and master a selection of basic online life skills dealing with issues of communication online, including the cyber threat of predators. Sections include:

5.1.   Online Identity Basics

5.2.   Online Strangers, Predators, and the Grooming Process

5.3.   Willing Participation

5.4.   The Future of the Internet and YOU

5.5.   Enrichment Activity—Wrap It Up!

5.6.   Unit Review

In addition to written activities, lesson sections include:

- **Learning Objectives:** List of the expected outcomes of what you are to understand upon completion of the lesson. Use the learning objectives to get a preview of lesson content before the lesson and as a guide to what you will be expected to know on the unit quiz.

- **Terms to Know:** Learn and practice critical terms and definitions associated with the lesson topic.

- **Think About It—Talk About It:** Thought-provoking questions to consider that, depending on classroom setup, can be directed to think about independently or discuss at home, with a partner, in a small group, or as a class.

• **Cyber Know-How:** Resource and/or skill-based information.

 • **Cyber Tales:** Stories of real experiences on the "Net."

 • **Free Write:** Exploration of the topics through a writing prompt and space to jot down thoughts and previous knowledge.

 • **Use What U Have Learned:** Directed or self-guided activity to support and/or demonstrate learning.

 • **Online Extension:** Activities set up by the instructor to go online and apply what has been learned, either by researching a topic or completing a task.

 • **Reaching Others:** Guidance for extending what has been learned by sharing information with others.

Additional Resources

Your instructor may provide you with additional online and/or offline resources to complete these activities.

Learning Objectives

Students will:

- Understand basic identity risk issues associated with Internet use
- Demonstrate how to make a safe password
- Identify examples of risky behavior in online communications

 ## Terms to Know

- anonymous
- appropriate
- inappropriate
- indirect
- non-identifying
- personal information
- profile
- screen name
- user ID

Use the "terms to know" above to fill in the blanks and create true sentences. Use each word only once.

1. Online posting of one's characteristics or qualities make up his or her online _____ .

2. _____ and _____ both mean online nickname or identity.

3. If an online identity is unsuitable or improper, we say that it is _____ .

4. Many people think they are completely _____ while online, but unfortunately just being connected to the Internet provides identifying information about the user.

5. _____ describes a person's identity such as name, date of birth, address, etc.

6. It is _____ for people to use the Internet for education, recreation, and socializing if done safely.

7. The use of _____ terms for screen names and user IDs is one way to maintain a safe profile online.

8. It may signal danger if someone tries to get personal information from another in an _____ way.

Think About It—Talk About It

Although it sometimes seems like it, you do not have complete anonymity when you are on the Internet. When you log on, others have access to you. Your e-mail address, screen name, and password serve as barriers between you and others. You need to maintain this barrier by guarding your private information. Every time you give out bits of personal information, you become less anonymous—easier to identify!

Unfortunately, there are many out there who would like to know more about you for a variety of reasons, including:

- They could want to harm you physically.
- They could want to steal from you.
- They could use information to conduct their own business, either by selling your information or by using it in an illegal manner.

Cyber Know-How

Your screen name(s) and user ID(s) represent you in Cyberspace. It's fun to send a message or portray an image with a screen name. However, when you create a screen name, you want something that allows you to remain anonymous, or unknown, to anyone you don't want your identity revealed to.

- In order to protect your identity in the physical world, online screen/user names should never include personal or identifying information, including (but not limited to):
  - Your real first and last name
  - Any part of your address
  - Your location (i.e., Chicagogirl, HaverhillGuy)
  - Your telephone number
  - Your e-mail address
- Do not use an inappropriate suggestive name or word to describe yourself (i.e., sexyman42, hotbabygirl). You may attract the wrong kind of people.
- Do not use pornographic or obscene words.
- Be careful that you don't COMBINE pieces of personal information with other information that can be used to identify you or your location, such as in the screen name MJSmith95070.

 # Use What U Have Learned

Create an appropriate screen name for each of the people described below:

Robert Fairfax: Fifteen years old; lives in Cincinnati, Ohio; likes to skateboard; eat pizza, phone number is 507-555-3216; e-mail address is robert15@mailbox.net

Screen name: _____

Joni Drew: Twelve years old; has had a lot of stage experience (singing, dancing, and in plays); dreams of being a rock star; lives in Los Angeles; owns five cats

Screen name: _____

Kaimi Chang: Fourteen years old; lives in Seattle; likes to draw and paint; estimates that she spends more than twenty-five hours a week online; has profiles on four different social-networking sites

Screen name: _____

Jared Campbell: Thirteen years old; lives in Kentucky; has four brothers; likes to work on cars; can't wait to get a driver's license; will graduate in the year 2012

Screen name: _____

Online Profiles

A common Internet safety tip is: "Never give out personal information online."

And as a matter of fact, it is against the law for Web sites to ask for personal, identifying information from anyone thirteen years old or younger. However, sometimes we all need to post some personal information in online profiles to be able to use the Internet for good purposes. Your "online profile" provides the information that you submit to describe yourself. This can be as in an online profile form that you fill out to enroll in a service such as IM or a social network.

It is wise to keep in mind that most online profiles ask for much more information than is required. Required information is usually indicated by an asterisk (*) or the word "required." If you must complete an online profile, it is safest to fill in required information only.

Check out the privacy settings on any Web site you plan to put personal information on. It may not seem interesting to do this, but knowing what a Web site does

with your information and/or ways you can keep your information from being public will help to keep your identity secure.

 **Use What U Have Learned**

Check out this profile and circle all of the unsafe information.

Jackson's Profile

Name: Jackson Anderson

Age: 15

Sex: Male

Location: San Diego, California

Schools: San Diego High School
2006-2009

Music: Just sounds produced by vocals, guitars, basses, and drums...

Television: The Simpsons, South Park, MTV

Movies: Transformers, Blades of Glory, Stars Wars

Books: Redwulf's Curse, The Cry of Icemark

Heroes: My Mom

Groups: Soccer Team, Boys and Girls Club

Status: Single

Orientation: Straight

Hometown: San Diego

Body Type: 4" 6'

Zodiac Sign: Pisces

Smoke/Drink: No/No

Children: Undecided

Education: High School

Religion: Christian

Here for: Networking, Friends

Ethnicity: Caucasian

Think Out of the Box!

List safety strategies and/or ideas that you came up with to make this profile safer. For example, using initials instead of full name, etc.

In the blank profile below, re-create Jackson's profile to be safer.

Jackson's Profile

Name:

Age:

Sex:

Location:

Schools:

Music:

Television:

Movies:

Books:

Heroes:

Groups:

Status:

Orientation:

Hometown:

Body Type:

Zodiac Sign:

Smoke/Drink:

Children:

Education:

Religion:

Here for:

Ethnicity:

Think About It

- Does any of your personal/identifying information already exist in online profiles?
- Are all of your online profiles necessary for the activities you normally do online, or can one or more be deleted?
- How much information about yourself have you made public in online conversations?

 # Cyber Know-How

There is more than one meaning for the term "profile" when we are talking about Cyberspace. "Online profile" can also mean the picture of yourself that you paint every time you describe something personal about yourself in an online forum such as in a chat, in an e-mail, on a blog, in an IM, or on a Web site.

Indirect Information Solicitation

Sometimes people can find out all about you "indirectly"—by piecing bits of seemingly unrelated information together. For example, simple questions about your name, school, activities, etc., provide indirect information that could lead someone to figure out where you live.

How? Once a stranger knows a few bits of information, he or she can find your school location, then look up your last name up in a phone book to obtain the address. A simple online map search will even provide an aerial view of your neighborhood.

Online and Out of Your Control—You Can't Take it Back!

Have you ever thought about what happens or can happen to your personal information in Cyberspace?

Brainstorm a list of things that might happen to personal information as soon as it is placed online.

_____

_____

_____

_____

What did you come up with?

Once you post something online, it is available to other people and to search engines. You can change or remove information from a profile that has been available online, but it is possible that someone has already seen the original version and has copied the information. In the case of photos this can be a real problem because your photo can be edited by someone else and used for purposes that you do not intend.

Online communication is a real problem if you want to delete something you have said about yourself. Unless you run the webpage or blog where the information is located, it is virtually impossible to get rid of what has been revealed. Information on the Internet can remain for years and years. Additionally, some search engines "cache" copies of webpages so that they open faster; these cached copies may be available after a webpage has been deleted or altered. Some Web browsers may also maintain a cache of the webpages a user has visited, so the original version may be stored in a temporary file on the user's computer.

Don't even think about controlling something after you click "SEND." Messaging and e-mails are public as soon as they reach the message receiver.

> **Best Advice**
>
> Use common sense and think about these implications before you post information online. Once something is out there, you can't guarantee that you can remove it completely.

Activity—Sample Chat

Circle the unsafe behaviors and identities in this chat transcript. Briefly describe why it is unsafe in the space next to that line.

Members of the Chat

JAYHOOD21	Leann
brandon18sgirl	Angeleyes15
Andrew15MGA	ladybug16
zpencer2k3	

Online Chat

JAYHOOD21: So wuz everybody up 2?

Andrew15MGA: Not much here. Just got back from the game. We won 14 to 3. Way to go BRUINS!

Leann: How cool, my school's mascot is stupid. It's the Mustangs.

Angeleyes15: I'm at a private school. We don't even have a mascot cuz no sports. We focus on "academics." I really hate it.

zpencer2k3: I'm at a private school too. What one do you go to Angeleyes?

Angeleyes15: It's in Tampa, Florida.

ladybug16: How cool. I'm from Florida too.

zpencer2k3: Me too.

brandon18sgirl: I wish I lived in Florida. Its freezing here.

Andrew15MGA: Who saw "Buffy" last night? She is so hot!

Leann: I wish I was blonde.

Angeleyes15: Trust me it's not that much fun. With my blue eyes I burn too easy.

zpencer2k3: You go to the beach a lot?

Angeleyes15: All the time.

zpencer2k3: Maybe we could meet up at the Clearwater beach sometime. It's my favorite hangout lately.

Angeleyes15: Sounds kewl. I think I can get a ride down there.

 **Cyber Know-How**

Did you find everything in the sample chat on the previous page? Compare your answers to the ones below. You may have found things that are not listed here!

Members of the Chat

JAYHOOD21	Has name in it and potential age
brandon18sgir	Reveals friend/boyfriends name and gender
Andrew15MGA	Reveals first name and age
zpencer2k3	Reveals last name
Leann	Reveals first name
Angeleyes15	Possible age
ladybug16	Possible age

Online Chat

JAYHOOD21: So wuz everybody up 2?

Andrew15MGA: Not much here. Just got back from the game. We won 14 to 3. Way to go BRUINS! [Reveals indirect information leading to location—score and mascot could help pinpoint location.]

Leann: How cool, my school's mascot is stupid. It's the Mustangs. [Mascot helps determine or narrow down location.]

Angeleyes15: I'm at a private school. We don't even have a mascot cuz no sports. We focus on "academics." I really hate it. [Some indirect information can be built upon—now know private school with no sports or mascot.]

zpencer2k3: I'm at a private school too. What one do you go to Angeleyes? [Private school revealed.]

Angeleyes15: It's in Tampa, Florida. [Big mistake—reveals exact location in answer to question.]

ladybug16: How cool. I'm from Florida too. [Also reveals general location.]

zpencer2k3: Me too. [Also reveals general location.]

brandon18sgirl: I wish I lived in Florida. Its freezing here. [Implies location in the north.]

Andrew15MGA: Who saw "Buffy" last night? She is so hot! [Favorite TV show revealed.]

Leann: I wish I was blonde. [Color of hair hinted at.]

Angeleyes15: Trust me it's not that much fun. With my blue eyes I burn too easy. [Reveals color of hair and eyes.]

zpencer2k3: You go to the beach a lot?

Angeleyes15: All the time. [Reveals beach going.]

zpencer2k3: Maybe we could meet up at the Clearwater beach sometime. It's my favorite hangout lately. [Reveals favorite place to go.]

Angeleyes15: Sounds kewl. I think I can get a ride down there. [Responds positively to suggestion of meeting]

Instant communication can result in providing information you wouldn't normally reveal. This can leave you open to harm.

- Keep online interaction online. Don't agree to meet or phone people met online.
- Protect your personal information. Be careful about indirectly saying too much about yourself. Eventually you will have said enough.
- Private chats aren't always private. When you meet offline friends online in a private chat room, be careful. Others can often enter and lurk (watch what you are saying about yourself).

Make your own cartoon

Learning Objectives

- Define an online stranger as anyone met exclusively online
- List safety rules/advice of behavior toward strangers in the physical community that also apply to behavior toward strangers in Cyberspace
- Recognize steps in an online predator's grooming process
- Recognize how to respond appropriately/safely to Internet strangers

 Cyber Tale

This is a true story about a thirteen-year-old girl from Texas. We'll call her Kelly.

Kelly met a person in a chat room who had the same interests in life that she did. Kelly and her cyber friend talked online for about a month before deciding to meet each other in person. This was an exciting time for Kelly—to finally get to meet "Rick"!

Kelly's friend had a special surprise for her. He paid for a taxi to go to her house and pick her up when her parents weren't home. He had convinced Kelly that it would be a lot easier to keep things a secret from friends and family—just too many questions to have to answer! The taxi took her to the bus station, where there was a pre-paid ticket waiting for her.

Kelly rode the bus for 2½ days to Tacoma, Washington, where her cyber friend met her at the bus station. For the next five days, Kelly says she was assaulted repeatedly. Fortunately, she was able to call an emergency number that helped her get back to her family.

It is interesting to note that, before she left, Kelly's friend gave her instructions on how to remove the hard drive from her computer. This made tracing the "cyber friend" virtually impossible.

Kelly could have prevented this from ever happening if she had known the right information to keep her safe online.

Activity

List possible reasons why Kelly considered Rick to be a trustworthy friend.

_____

_____

_____

What are possible reasons why Kelly didn't recognize Rick's willingness to pay for her transportation as a danger signal?

_____

_____

_____

What are possible reasons why Kelly didn't recognize Rick's asking her to remove her computer hard drive as a danger signal?

_____

_____

_____

Why do you think Kelly willingly participated in a relationship that eventually harmed her?

_____

_____

_____

Predators and Prey

Let's define "online predator."

- Think about what the word "predator" means to you. Does the word make you think of lions hunting for their next meal?

- A predator is one who stalks or uses lies, secrecy, or stealth to get close enough to another person in order to easily hurt or harm him or her.

- Now think about what the word "prey" means to you.

- "Prey" is one who is a victim or one who is vulnerable to victimization by a predator (the lion's meal!).

We also use these words in terms of the Internet.

- Some people lie about who they are and what they want on the Internet for various reasons.

- Sometimes it is to steal an identity or to bully.

160 Unit 5: A Common-Sense Approach to Strangers Online (5–8)

- Other times it is to meet children and teens to form an inappropriate relationship.
- These people are known as "online predators." The people who are the intended victims are the "prey."

The Grooming Process

It's a fact that anyone met exclusively online (not a known friend from the physical community) is a stranger. Some people lie about who they are and what they want on the Internet for various reasons. Sometimes it is to steal an identity or to bully. Other times it is to meet children and teens to form an inappropriate relationship.

Consider the following statistics obtained from a survey of students before they learned about Internet safety:

- More than 74 percent of fifth graders spent at least an hour online each week.
- 50 percent of fifth graders spend time in chat rooms.
- More than 7 percent of those in fifth grade have met someone face-to-face they met online.

Finding the perfect prey . . .

Predators generally tend to target kids:

- Who are lonely and have easy Internet access
- Who spend more than three hours a day online
- Who are online during the hours when their parents aren't home
- Who have better technology skills than their parents have

 Think About It—Talk About It

You may not be lonely, but how do you measure up to the list above?

According to law enforcement experts, predators almost always pose as teenagers at first, using fake pictures and phony online profiles. Once they've gained the victim's trust, they slowly reveal their true age.

Would you know whether someone else's profile was a fake?

What Do You Think?

Fact or Fiction? Cyber predators are only a problem for girls.

Although there may be fewer public stories about boys being victimized, everyone needs to be aware that cyber predators target boys as well as girls. This is proven every time law enforcement officers pose online in "sting" operations designed to catch cyber predators.

A typical example: Under the screen name "BIG PAPA," a thirty-five-year-old predator we'll call "Smith" started chatting online with an investigator posing as a thirteen-year-old Florida boy. Within minutes, Smith was asking to meet, and he actually traveled to meet the "boy" less than twenty-four hours after meeting him online.

The Grooming Process

How can you be sure who you're talking to online? Internet predators use what is known as "the grooming process" to create seemingly safe online relationships and then betray the friendship by attempting to break down barriers and cause harm.

> Online predators find victims by going to chat rooms where young people gather or by searching online profiles for the type of victim they are looking for.

Predators use a process to groom their victims that usually follows this pattern:

1. **Establish Similar Interests** through chatting or instant messaging. This leads to more private communication like e-mail and phone calls.

2. **Build Trust.** A predator counts on the fact that establishing so much in common with an online friend will lead to a trusting relationship. A predator is hoping that you will develop such a trust that you will separate yourself from your true friends and family.

3. **Keep It a Secret.** It is a predator's goal to make the friendship a secret from others. Engaging in a secret friendship like this leaves you vulnerable to harm.

4. **Break Down Barriers.** A predator works on the trust that has been established and may break down barriers further by exposing the victim to pictures or materials that may at first make him or her uncomfortable. This is a common tactic because kids and teens are

naturally curious about many things. The more a victim is exposed to, the less he or she will feel that it is wrong.

5. **Make Threats.** Sometimes, but not always, a predator will make threats to the intended victim to keep the relationship a secret. Online threats are against the law. Think about it— would a real friend threaten you or your family with harm?

6. **Meet Face-to-Face.** The ultimate goal of an Internet predator is to get the intended victim to meet with him or her in person. You may believe that you can never be tricked by someone you meet online, but remember that predators make it their business to learn tactics to deceive their prey. NEVER meet anyone in person you only know online.

Best Advice

Online friendships can be fun, but always consider what kind of information you are sharing.

If you notice that one of your online friendships is following the grooming process pattern, proceed very cautiously. There is no reason for an online friend to want to have a secret relationship with you and/or to force you to meet in person.

Let your friends and family know about people you meet online and tell someone immediately if you are threatened or feel uncomfortable about anything that is said or sent online.

Put It Together

Think back to the story about Kelly on page 159.

List the steps of the grooming process Kelly's cyber friend used and briefly describe each.

_____

_____

_____

_____

_____

_____

Kelly's story ends with the following:

"Kelly could have prevented this from ever happening if she had known the right information to keep her safe online."

If you could have taught Kelly enough to save her from having this experience, what would it have been?

_____

_____

_____

_____

 ## Cyber Know-How

Minimizing Danger from Online Predators

There are things you can do to minimize the danger and the chances of becoming prey to an online predator. These safety precautions include choosing a safe screen name, not revealing too much information on the Internet, and carefully choosing whom to communicate with. No matter what, it is important to tell a trusted adult, such as a parent or teacher, if you ever feel uncomfortable online or are approached by someone who discusses inappropriate things or wants to meet you offline.

Use What U Have Learned

Your friend keeps telling you about her online friend. Lately the online friend has been sending e-mails asking to meet at the movies alone. Put into your own words what you would tell your friend about to handle this situation safely.

_____

_____

_____

_____

_____

Learning Objectives

- Understand the concept of willing participation
- Understand the safety risks of pursuing online relationships/friendships

 ## Think About It—Talk About It

Answer the questions below and discuss with a student group if directed by your teacher.

1. Why do you go online? Circle all that apply and/or add reasons not listed:

   boredom, play games, make friends, do homework, chat, IM, learn about things

2. How do you determine the age of people online?

   _____

   _____

3. Would you hide an online friendship from others?

   _____

   _____

4. Do you add people to your buddy list when online?

   _____

   _____

5. Do you "personally know" everyone on your buddy list?

   _____

   _____

6. In your opinion, when does being friends with someone online become "inappropriate"?

   _____

   _____

7. Do you know of any friends, either online or offline, who have online relationships that they keep secret?

   _____

   _____

Cyber Tales: True Story Script

Christina: My name is Christina. I'm fourteen years old and, you know, I guess I'm pretty normal. I live in Danbury, Connecticut. I go to a private school and I'm on the cheerleading squad. Go Titans! Last semester I got all A's and a B. Algebra is not my thing. On weekends I like to go to the Danbury Fair Mall with my friends and hang out.

Saul: My name is Saul. I'm from a small town in Brazil but grew up and went to school in the U.S. I like to go into chat rooms and talk to young girls about things that interest them. I like to use chat rooms because I can hide who I am and can talk about anything I want. My screen name is Hot ES 300, named after my Lexus. You see, I like to chat with girls who have the same interests as I do.

Christina: I really like chatting online. I've met a lot of cool people that way. Kids who like what I like. Sometimes when I'm feeling alone I turn on the computer and see who's chatting. I can sit in my room and chat online for hours. I met one of my best friends online. It all started with IM. It's weird, but we totally like the same things so we have a lot to talk about. His screen name is Hot ES 300 and he's from Rhode Island. I can talk to him about anything, school, guys, and my family. I have friends, but I've never had a friend like him. It's different because I can talk to him about everything, even my other friends.

Saul: One afternoon in April of 2000 I was instant messaging various people who have similar interests as me and began to chat with a girl whose screen name was Long 2 hot 4 u. Her real name is Christina Long from Danbury, Connecticut. Our similar interests were fast cars. We also liked to flirt with each other.

Christina: We started chatting about cars and pretty soon we were talking about all kinds of other stuff, personal stuff. He really gets me. No one really knows about him, which is cool. It's like this thing that's totally just between us. He told me that if I told my aunt she might worry so I should just keep everything between us. He's right, she would probably freak if she knew that I talked to him on the phone last week.

Saul: Today is May 17th and I am going to meet her at the mall. I cannot wait until tonight. It is going to be a night we will never forget.

Christina: He wants to meet me at the mall. He's driving from Rhode Island just to take me to dinner next Saturday. I'm really excited to meet him. I know exactly what I'm going to wear and I'm sure he is going to like it.

Continued

Saul: What she doesn't know is that I am going to take her in my car and strangle her to death. I am going to dump her body in a ditch and lie to police just like I lied to her.

Saul: My name is Saul dos Reis. I am twenty-five years old. I am now sitting in an eight-foot-by-eight-foot cement room. I will be here for the next thirty years for the enticement, seduction, and for the murder of the girl I met online named Christina. . . .

Put It Together

- What are some safety/security risks Christina took when online?

_____

_____

_____

- What part did Christina's screen name play in the development of her relationship with Saul?

_____

_____

_____

- What part did Saul's screen name play in the development of her relationship with Christina?

_____

_____

_____

- List possible reasons why Christina considered Saul to be a trustworthy friend.

_____

_____

_____

- List ways that Saul "groomed" Christina to be his victim.

_____

_____

Remember
Always be
SAFE!!!

- Why do we call Christina a willing participant in the relationship?

_____

_____

Unit 5: A Common-Sense Approach to Strangers Online (5–8)   **167**

Your Turn

While online, have you ever been asked for your A/S/L? (Age/Sex/Location)

How did you respond?

_____

_____

_____

_____

_____

Describe any unusual, suspicious, or scary experiences you have had when chatting or messaging with online people. What might their intentions have been? How did you handle it?

_____

_____

_____

_____

_____

Would you do anything different if it happened again?

_____

_____

_____

_____

_____

If you haven't had an actual experience, write a fictional story/experience that could happen to someone.

_____

_____

_____

_____

_____

How might others be able to learning from the experience(s) you described in the previous section?

_____

_____

_____

_____

_____

It's fun to meet and communicate with people on the Internet. And most of the time online friendships can be great when they stay ONLINE! When you engage in an online friendship with a stranger, you are considered to be a "willing participant."

Be Aware

It takes constant attention to detail to maintain a SAFE online friendship.

If anyone uses any of the steps of the grooming process on you or on one of your friends, be suspicious! A person who behaves in any of these ways is not behaving appropriately on the Internet, and he or she should not be considered to be any kind of friend.

Create a list of Internet safety tips that could help someone else be safer online.

- Identify an age group your tips are targeting if you have created them for younger or older youth.
- Make it REAL. Make your list fit the real-world behaviors and attitudes of kids and teens on the Internet—Cyberspace.
- Cover as many things as you can think of. You will use these tips in the enrichment activity.

_____

_____

_____

_____

_____

_____

 ## Think About It—Talk About It

Hundreds of thousands of students from all over the United States have taken i-SAFE's online surveys about Internet usage. The surveys tell us that, although there are some differences in the exact online activities that youth engage in depending on the area of the country they live in, we can get a general view of how today's youth are shaping the Internet of tomorrow. In other words, the types of things that become popular today have an impact on the type of technologies and activities that will be available in the future.

You are shaping Cyberspace!

Where Do You Want to Fit In?

Student surveys are compiled by the National Assessment Center (NAC). The results are very interesting. Read and reflect on the following.

Do you IM or text message?

Are "Buddy Lists" a status symbol? Students pad their lists with their classmates, their friends' friends, and anyone available to boast a large number. It is not uncommon to have ninety names on a "Buddy List," a good portion of which are strangers.

According to a NAC survey of 123,000 students in grades five through twelve:

- 32 percent admit to using the Internet unsafely, inappropriately, or illegally.
- 22 percent of students in grades three through twelve open e-mails from strangers.
- 20 percent would classify someone they meet only on the Internet as a "very good friend."
- 57 percent of all fifth- through twelfth-graders are members of various online social networking Web sites like Facebook, MySpace, Xanga, etc.
- 15 percent of all respondents in grades five through twelve indicated that they would be willing to meet face-to-face with someone they first met on the Internet.

Many students post personal information on their webpages that could assist a stranger to identify or locate them. Nearly half (49 percent) of students in grades nine through twelve and almost one-third (31 percent) of students in grades five through eight have done so. Among students with a personal blog, 43 percent of high school students and one in four (24 percent) middle school students have posted photos of themselves on theirs. About one in six (16 percent) of all third and fourth graders have photos of themselves posted online.

- 50 percent of high school students "talk" in chat rooms or use instant messaging (IM) with Internet strangers.
- 13 percent of students in grades five through eight have shared personal information with someone they had only just met on the Internet.

- 12 percent of students in middle and high school admit that they have met face-to-face with someone they first met on the Internet.

- In the summer of 2007 it was reported that managers of a popular social networking site found and deleted the profiles of more than 29,000 registered sex offenders.

You have the opportunity to become a part of the NAC. Ask your teacher about how and when to complete the i-SAFE online assessments at http://www.isafe.org.

Free Write—You Are Shaping Cyberspace!

Considering what you have learned, how do you think the behaviors of youth and cyber predators may shape the Internet of the future? For example:

- Do you think the current freedoms enjoyed on the Internet will change? If so, how will they change? New laws? Restricted access to Web sites?
- Do you want to see change? Why or why not?
- In your opinion, what kinds of things need to be done by adults to make the Internet a safer place?
- In your opinion, what kinds of things need to be done by youth to make the Internet a safer place?

_____

_____

_____

_____

_____

Online Extension

You have just written a short essay on youth behaviors, current freedoms, online laws, and more. Take the time now to share that essay with i-SAFE. You can submit your writing (300-word maximum) through e-mail to activitybook@isafe.org. i-SAFE will use these essays to spot behavioral trends, shape lessons, advocate for legislation, publish, use in teaching examples, and more. Writers will be anonymous if their works are chosen but are playing an important role and part in improving the future of the Internet. Share your writing with us now!

This section will lead you through the steps to create an informative brochure or flyer to help others who may be at risk of being a victim of an Internet predator.

Step 1. Identify your target audience. Who will benefit the most from the information you can provide—parents, students, public at large (or even all three!)?

Step 2. Gather information. With your target audience in mind, review this book. Use reference information and activities you have completed in the previous pages to create the content of your brochure. Use the space on the following page to collect the information.

Step 3. Organize the information into a format. For example:
- Will it be a one-page flyer, a folded brochure?
- Will you create graphics/artwork?
- What will the title be?

Step 4. Use materials of choice (handwritten/designed or with the use of desktop publishing) to design and create brochures.

Step 5. Make plans to copy the brochure(s) and distribute. Figure out where the brochure will have the most impact. Plan distribution there (distribute in cafeteria at lunch, after a parent open house, during a faculty meeting, etc.)
- Make sure you have permission for your distribution.
- Check with your teacher for ideas, too.

Step 6. Copy brochures.

Step 7. Plan a distribution day.

Step 8. Distribute brochures.

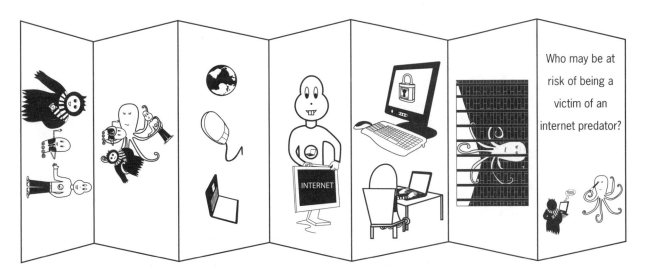

Who may be at risk of being a victim of an internet predator?

Unit 5: A Common-Sense Approach to Strangers Online (5–8) **173**

Brochure Content

Organize information you want to publish in your brochure or flyer here.

Include important information or other ideas.

_____

_____

_____

_____

_____

_____

_____

_____

_____

_____

_____

_____

_____

_____

_____

_____

_____

_____

_____

Safety Tips

_____

_____

_____

_____

1. Of the following, the best way to protect your online profile is to:
   a. Give only your street name, not the house address
   b. Never post a home phone number
   c. Enable privacy settings
   d. List fake hobbies and interests

2. What can happen to personal information that is posted publicly online for a short time?
   a. The information can be saved by others for future use
   b. Location can be identified
   c. Picture can be altered and/or sent to others via e-mail without permission
   d. All of the above

3. Which of the following examples could be steps in a predator's grooming process? (Select all that apply.)
   a. Stays online chatting with you for three hours to make you feel better after having a fight with your parents.
   b. Sends an electronic gift certificate
   c. Names a date and time where s/he can be met at the mall
   d. Introduces you to another friend who has the same interests as you

4. Which of the following screen names is the safest?
   a. alex
   b. alexsmith
   c. alexintx
   d. alex14

5. Which statement is true?
   a. According to surveys, less than 50 percent of youth in grades five through twelve are members of online social networking Web sites.
   b. According to surveys, about one-fourth of middle-school students have posted photos of themselves on personal Web sites.
   c. Children in grade three and four do not communicate much online.
   d. These days social networking networks are safer because they are required by law to keep registered sex offenders from using their Web sites.

6. Which statement is false?
   a. When you engage in an online friendship with a stranger, you are considered to be a "willing participant."
   b. Cyber predators target boys as well as girls.

c. The online activities popular today have an impact on the types of Internet technologies that will be available in the future.

d. A way to combine personal information in a screen name safely is to use your first name with your birth date or age.

7. Someone met only online should always be considered a stranger. True or false?
   a. true
   b. false

8. Most forms of social networking should be avoided because it is unsafe. True or false?
   a. true
   b. false

9. Adults do not need to worry about keeping their personal information private on the Internet. True or False?
   a. true
   b. false

10. A secret online friendship is safe if you make sure you remain anonymous. True or False?
    a. true
    b. false

Unit 6: Cyber Citizenship and Netiquette Sense (5–8)

Unit Goal

Throughout the lesson/activities, learners will develop an understanding of the concept of "netiquette" and how it applies to online behaviors and interactions.

Understanding the Unit Format

This guide will provide you with discussion guidance, answers to activity questions, and an explanation of the content of the student pages.

Cyber Citizenship and Netiquette Sense lesson/activity sections include:

6.1. Rules, Laws, and Ethics
6.2. Understanding Netiquette
6.3. Cyber Bullying and Netiquette Sense
6.4. Enrichment Activity—Wrap It Up!
6.5. Unit Review

Additional Resources

Refer to the i-SAFE *i-EDUCATOR Times* newsletters located at www.isafe.org and general i-SAFE lesson plans on similar topics for additional resource materials and background information if needed.

Prepare for the Lesson

Pre-Assessment

- If beginning the i-SAFE program with this unit, administer the pre-assessment online at http://www.isafe.org/activitybook.
- Enter School ID# 24615.

Post-Assessment

- If you will end the i-SAFE program with this unit, have students complete the post-assessment online at http://www.isafe.org/activitybook.
- Students complete the Outcomes assessment three to six weeks after completion of the last i-SAFE lesson implemented.

Plan Your Format

This unit is designed to enable transition from traditional class lessons to a more self-guided format, depending on student reading abilities.

1. Arrange for students to take the online pre-assessment.
2. Review the student activity pages and determine how you will implement the unit.
3. *Optional:* Prepare any additional reference material of your choice, including Internet access.
4. Provide each student with a copy of the student pages and review directions for student use.

Implementation Options

The following are suggested options for implementing the unit.

Group guided: Use the activities as short lessons over a period of time (one or two weeks to complete). This option is especially recommended for students with less developed reading comprehension skills.

- Have students complete the online pre-assessment prior to engaging in the i-SAFE program.
- Assign and go over each activity page with the class as a large group and have students complete them as instructed. You may want to have students read over text parts together to reinforce meaning.
- Go over completed pages with the group as they are finished.
- Have students complete the online post-assessment.
- Complete the empowerment activity suggested, or create your own activity.

Small groups: Students work in groups to complete the activities. This may be done in several sessions.

- Have students complete the online pre-assessment prior to engaging in the i-SAFE program.
- Introduce the unit with the pre-activity discussion.

- Create small work groups of three to four students.
- Student groups complete the assigned pages for each session and discuss their answers within the group.
- Go over the Wrap-Up activity to review the concepts presented in the unit.
- Have students complete the online post-assessment.
- Complete the empowerment activity suggested, or create your own activity.

Semi-self-guided: This option should only be considered for age-proficient readers. Create a timeline for activities to be completed.

- Have students complete the online pre-assessment prior to engaging in the i-SAFE program.
- Introduce the unit with the Activity 1 discussion.
- Have students complete their assignments.
- Go over the Wrap-Up activity to review the concepts.
- Have students complete the online post-assessment.
- Complete the empowerment activity suggested, or create your own activity.

6.1. Rules, Laws, and Ethics (page 189)

Introduce the Unit

- Have a student read the introduction out loud.
- As a class, go over the explanations of the sections in "Understanding the Activities."
- Have students complete the activities according to the implementation format you have chosen.

Terms to Know Definitions

- Citizenship—the quality of a person's response to membership in a community.
- Conduct (noun)—personal behavior.
- Ethics—sets of values based on concepts of right and wrong.
- Laws—rules of conduct/behavior established by custom, agreement or authority.
- Obligation—something one must do (promise or contract to do something).
- Rules—guides for conduct or action.

Think About It—Talk About It Answer Key

There are many possible answers, including the following: Laws—traffic laws, laws against stealing, laws against crimes (list). Laws are in place to keep citizens safe and create and orderly environment.

Expectations for good citizenship include: helping others in need, being polite, keeping the environment clean, etc.

Put it Together Answer Key

Answers may include the following.

It is illegal to do the following online:

- Hack into Web sites
- Steal intellectual property
- Threaten others

Go Online Answer Key

Define Cyber Ethics (Definitions should include concepts that reflect the relationship of social and moral issues in the physical world to those in Cyberspace.)

6.2. Understanding Netiquette (page 193)

Terms to Know Answer Key

- Acronym—a word formed from the initial letters of the several words in the name.
- Evolve—to develop and move forward.
- Netiquette—etiquette for the Internet, for example: respecting others' privacy and not doing anything online that will annoy or frustrate other people.
- Polite—showing consideration and courtesy.
- Rude—lacking education, ill-mannered, discourteous.

Cyber Know-How Answer Key

Why is it easy to forget one is interacting with real people when online? (Perceived anonymity [feeling anonymous]; you can't see people you are communicating with.)

What types of issues can "forgetting" cause? (It is easier to say mean things or give out personal information that one would probably not consider saying face-to-face.)

Texting Know-How Answer Key

- Watch your tone. Clarify what you mean by using emoticons like smiley faces, etc. (Without seeing a person's facial expressions or hearing his or her tone of voice, text communication makes it harder to identify a message as, for instance, a joke or a mean remark.)
- Don't use offensive language. (Use of offensive language encourages others to respond in a similar way, ultimately creating an environment that is offensive.)
- Don't use ALL CAPITAL LETTERS all of the time. (Using all caps is considered to be shouting on the Internet and can be taken the wrong way by the reader.)
- Identify appropriate use (or policies) for online areas or activities you engage in. (Answers will vary.)
- Always use your own online identity, not someone else's. (Using another's identity can set that person up for abusive or criminal actions.)
- Stay away from the flames (angry, rude, or offensive messages/postings are known as flames). (This type of behavior encourages others to respond in a similar way, ultimately creating an environment that is offensive.)
- Don't spam. Think carefully before forwarding e-mails or messages. (Spam slows down networks and can spread computer viruses.)
- Think before you text. (You can't take a sent message back. Rude, offensive, or angry messages can destroy relationships.)
- Help out newcomers. Everyone is new at some point. Helping others promotes good citizenship

Judge and Jury Answer Key

Instructions: Read this IM session between two friends. Can you find the netiquette errors?

Christy: Hey, did you hear what happened to Megan at school today?

Jeff: No, fill me in!

Christy: I heard she flipped out completely and had to be restrained until the police showed up. **Netiquette error: could be gossiping ("I heard . . . .")**

Jeff: Wow, I always did think she was freaky. She and Mike both—just a little too weird for me.

Christy: I don't know, Mike ain't that bad.

Jeff: I can't wait to let Sue know about Megan. I'm IMing her now. **Netiquette error: Spreading the gossip.**

Christy: Yeah just don't say I told. Do that and I won't ever fill you in again.

Jeff: YEAH YEAH, GO JUMP! **Netiquette error: All CAPS—rude comment.**

Christy: Hey, I just checked out your profile. Never looked at it before—cool pic. **Netiquette error: Profiles should not contain pictures or personal info.**

Jeff: Thanks. Yeah, I checked yours before—that's how I got hold of your e-mail address.

Christy: Cool. Steve just sent me a file to download. I met Steve online through Sue. Not sure how she met him. You ever talk to him? **Netiquette error: Downloading file from stranger.**

Jeff: Nope, don't know him. So what did he send you?

Christy: Looks like some pics and a game to install. **Netiquette error: May have a virus.**

Jeff: Be sure to send it on to me. I might send it to a few other people on my buddy list. **Netiquette error: Sending potentially dangerous files—spam.**

Put It Together

For each age group below, create a netiquette tip for using interactive technologies (Web 2.0). Possible answers:

Interactive Web sites for children up through age twelve:

- Treat people kindly.

Interactive Web sites for teenagers:

- Use appropriate language.

Interactive Web sites for adults:

- Do not post inappropriate photos.

6.3. Cyber Bullying and Netiquette Sense (page 199)

Terms to Know Definitions

- Bully—a person who hurts, is mean, frightens, or makes others feel bad physically or mentally through their actions and comments.
- Cyber harassment—using the Internet, cell phones, or other devices to send or post text or images intended to hurt or embarrass another person or in other ways attempt to harm.
- Inadvertent—happening by chance or unexpectedly or unintentionally.
- Threaten—present a danger to.

Think About It—Talk About It

Encourage discussion of the questions in this section

- How is cyber bullying/harassment a violation of basic cyber citizenship and freedom on the Internet?
- Why do some people react in extreme ways to "just words"?

Online and Helpless Activity

Students complete the Online and Helpless Activity by writing a helpful response to each letter. Each response should include information on appropriate netiquette knowledge and/or outside sources and tips on how similar problems might be avoided in the future.

If possible, have students discuss their answers.

Cyber Tales—It's the Law

Answers will be subjective.

Online Extension

Part 1: Research laws that address cyber bullying in your state. Write a paragraph in the space below to summarize what you found.

Helpful Links

- http://www.cyberbullyalert.com/blog/2008/10/cyber-bullying-state-laws-and-policies/
- http://www.ncsl.org/default.aspx?tabid=12903

Part 2: Research your school's anti-bullying policy and write a paragraph that explains how (or if) the policy addresses cyber bullying. Examples to include: where a student or parent can read the policy (Is it on the school Web site?); who should report bullying; how to report bullying and/or cyber bullying at school and who to report it to; consequences for bullies; whether your school district publishes district bullying policies on its Web site. (Does the school and district follow the law for your state?)

Hint: Cyber bullying policies are sometimes found in the school's Acceptable Use Policy (AUP).

Part 3: Research federal laws on cyber bullying. Write a paragraph that includes what you found out and your opinion on how well the government is addressing the issue.

6.4. Enrichment Activity—Wrap It Up (page 207)

Help students organize, set up, and monitor a D.R.O.P. box at the school.

Post-Assessment Reminder

- If you will end the i-SAFE program with this unit, have students complete the post-assessments online at http://www.isafe.org/activitybook.
- Students complete the Outcomes assessment three to six weeks after completion of the last i-SAFE lesson implemented.

6.5. Unit Review (page 209)

Instruct students when to complete the unit review.

Answers

1. c
2. b
3. d
4. b
5. c
6. a
7. b
8. d
9. c
10. b

It is impossible to think of life in today's world without the Internet. Cyberspace offers instant communication and seemingly infinite resources for all no matter the age, location, occupation, or interests a person might have. In fact, using the Internet is no longer an isolated factor that helps us with tasks; it is a complete society in which real people engage in everyday life. It is important to realize that one's online actions today can have a real impact on one's online presence in the future.

Understanding the Activities

These activities are designed to help you understand and master a selection of basic online life skills dealing with the topic of digital citizenship. Sections include:

6.1. Rules, Laws, and Ethics

6.2. Understanding Netiquette

6.3. Cyber Bullying and Netiquette Sense

6.4. Enrichment Activity—Wrap It Up!

6.5. Unit Review

In addition to written activities, lesson sections include:

- **Learning objectives:** List of the expected outcomes of what you are to understand upon completion of the lesson. Use the learning objectives to preview lesson content before the lesson and as a guide to what you will be expected to know on the unit quiz.

- **Terms to Know:** Learn and practice critical terms and definitions associated with the lesson topic.

- **Think About It—Talk About It:** Thought-provoking questions to consider that, depending on classroom setup, you can think about independently or discuss at home with a partner, in a small group, or as a class.

• **Cyber Know-How:** Resource and/or skill-based information.

 • **Cyber Tales:** Stories of real experiences on the "Net."

 • **Free Write:** Exploration of the topics through a writing prompt and space to jot down thoughts and previous knowledge.

 • **Use What U Have Learned:** Directed or self-guided activity to support and/or demonstrate learning.

 • **Online Extension:** Activities set up by the instructor to go online and apply what has been learned, either by researching a topic or completing a task.

 • **Reaching Others:** Guidance for extending what has been learned by sharing information with others.

Additional Resources

Your instructor may provide you with additional online and/or offline resources to complete these activities.

6.1. Rules, Laws, and Ethics

Learning Objectives

Upon completion of this section you should be able to:

- Assess and identify why ethics, rules and laws are needed when using digital technologies.
- Apply knowledge of ethics and rules to basic citizenship concepts.
- Identify ways one can be a good cyber citizen.

Terms to Know

Define the following words. Underline them and any words you don't know or are not sure of and use a dictionary to look them up.

- citizenship

_____

- conduct (noun)

_____

- ethics

_____

- laws

_____

- obligation

_____

- rules

_____

Think About It—Talk About It

The Internet is a community just like your physical community. In your physical community you have rules and laws you need to follow. What are some of these rules/laws? Why are these rules/laws in place?

_____

_____

_____

Beyond rules or guidelines and laws, identify at least two specific things you are "expected" to do or follow in order to be a good citizen in the physical community. How are these things different than rules or laws?

_____

_____

_____

Citizenship Know-How

A law is a rule of conduct or procedure established by custom, agreement, or authority. If a law is disobeyed (broken), a penalty is enforced. For example, the penalty for breaking a speed limit law while driving is usually a monetary fine.

Ethics are more vague. Poor ethical conduct, unless it involves breaking a law, carries no legal penalty. Ethics deal with good and bad, and moral duty or obligation.

Think About It

Who defines what is good or bad?

Typically, what is "ethically" right is determined by the large group or community. For example, it is ethically wrong to call people certain names that can hurt their feelings.

Sometimes ethics become rules, or laws, because everyone agrees with them. In other words, certain ethical behavior becomes the standard for a rule. For example, it is probably a rule in your school not to call people certain names.

Can you think of a law or rule that is based on a moral/ ethical standard? List it here:

_____

_____

_____

Becoming a good citizen is about following the rules, laws, and ethical standards of your area.

Put It Together

So how do we apply this to the Internet?

There are both state and federal laws that govern Internet activities, including laws that involve hacking into Web sites, music piracy, copyright issues, online gambling, and sending spam.

Use the following prompt to describe some laws you know of that apply to Internet activities. It is illegal to do the following online:

_____

_____

_____

Identify three reasons why some laws, rules or boundaries are necessary to ensure a positive Internet environment for its users.

_____

_____

_____

Now that you've thought about laws governing the online community, what about ethics?

_____

_____

_____

Free Write

What makes a good cyber citizen?

_____

_____

_____

_____

_____

_____

_____

_____

Go Online

- Do an Internet search to define the term, cyber ethics. (*Hint*: It is sometimes spelled as one word, cyberethics.)

- List at least two resources you found and then write a meaningful definition of the term.

_____

_____

_____

_____

_____

_____

_____

6.2. Understanding Netiquette

Learning Objectives

Upon completion of this section you should be able to:

- Define and apply basic netiquette skills to online interaction
- Describe how the use of netiquette skills promotes positive online experiences
- Understand the risks of not utilizing netiquette
- Use what has been learned to create netiquette tips for using interactive (Web 2.0) technologies

Terms to Know

- acronym
- evolve
- netiquette
- polite
- rude

Cyber Know-How

Netiquette is like a set of rules for polite behavior on the Internet. These are basic, widely accepted rules of behavior that have evolved over time. The use of netiquette positively affects the Internet environment by minimizing rude, offensive, or abusive online actions.

- Why is it easy to forget one is interacting with real people when online?

_____

_____

- What types of issues can "forgetting" cause?

_____

_____

Activity

Instructions: Think about what annoys you when you are online. What types of rules or guidelines would make your online experience a more positive (pleasant) one? Brainstorm your top five list of rules/guidelines that you would like people to follow when online:

1.

2.

3.

4.

5.

Texting Know-How

For each of the netiquette guidelines listed below, describe a reason why following this rule is important for maintaining a positive online experience. The first one is done for you as an example. Watch your tone. Clarify what you mean by using emoticons like smiley face, etc.

- Without seeing a person's facial expressions or hearing his or her tone of voice, text communication makes it harder to identify a message as, for instance, a joke or a mean remark.

Don't use offensive language.

_____

_____

_____

_____

Don't use ALL CAPITAL LETTERS all of the time.

_____

_____

_____

_____

Identify appropriate use (or policies) for online areas or activities you engage in.

_____

_____

_____

_____

Always use your own online identity, not someone else's.

_____

_____

_____

Stay away from the flames (angry, rude, or offensive messages/postings are known as flames).

_____

_____

_____

Don't spam. Think carefully before forwarding e-mails or messages.

_____

_____

_____

Think before you text.

_____

_____

_____

Help out newcomers.

_____

_____

_____

Now that you have some basic information about good cyber citizenship, let's take a look at two specific types of interactions. For each one, add any other rules you think are important. Then identify the one in the list that you think is the most important for creating a positive or safe/secure Internet environment, and tell why.

E-mail Netiquette

- Try to check e-mail regularly and respond appropriately.
- Don't forward messages.
- Delete messages as you read them.
- Don't send confidential information in e-mail. It can be intercepted/read by others.
- Proofread all e-mail messages.
- Don't send messages when angry or upset. Take time to calm down and reread.
- Respect others' privacy. Don't share e-mail addresses or messages without permission.
- Create a good subject line so others can quickly see what the e-mail is about.

_____

_____

Most important:

_____

_____

Text Messaging Netiquette

- Don't use offensive language.
- Don't send messages when angry or upset.
- Think before you send.

_____

_____

Most important:

_____

_____

Activity

The nature of online communication has resulted in new ways to convey feelings and emotions through acronyms and emoticons.

Acronyms: An abbreviation of several words in such a way to create a new word. For example, the acronym BRB stands for Be Right Back.

Emoticons: Short sequence of keyboard letters and symbols to represent a face, like the smiley face. Emoticons are used to show emotions in online communications.

Judge and Jury

Instant messaging (IM) can be lots of fun, but sometimes the jokes and humor in your messages can fall flat. Online conversations are different from real-world conversations. It's easy to be misunderstood online—especially if you're using putdowns or insults as humor—because the reader can't see your face or hear your tone of voice.

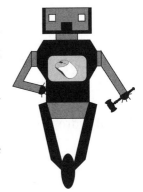

Instructions: Read this IM session between two friends. Can you find the netiquette errors? Fix the errors and add emoticons to show emotion.

Christy: Hey, did you hear what happened to Megan at school today?

_____

Jeff: No, fill me in!

_____

Christy: I heard she flipped out completely and had to be restrained until the police showed up.

_____

Jeff: Wow, I always did think she was freaky. She and Mike both—just a little too weird for me.

_____

Christy: I don't know. Mike ain't that bad.

_____

Jeff: I can't wait to let Sue know about Megan. I'm IMing her now.

_____

Christy: Yeah, just don't say I told. Do that and I won't ever fill you in again.

_____

Jeff: YEAH YEAH—GO JUMP!

_____

Christy: Hey, I just checked out your profile. Never looked at it before—cool pic.

_____

Jeff: Thanks. Yeah, I checked yours before—that's how I got hold of your e-mail address.

_____

Christy: Cool. Steve just sent me a file to download. I met Steve online through Sue. Not sure how she met him. You ever talk to him?

_____

Jeff: Nope, don't know him. So what did he send you?

_____

Christy: Looks like some pics and a game to install.

_____

Jeff: Be sure to send it on to me. I might send it to a few other people on my buddy list.

_____

Put It Together

Read the two statements below. Think about how statement 1 is related to statement 2; then complete the activity below.

Statement 1: Netiquette can be defined as widely accepted guidelines for polite behavior in Cyberspace that have evolved over time.

Statement 2: It has been said that netiquette guidelines have not kept up with the development of new interactive technologies, also called "Web 2.0" technologies, such as social networking sites and virtual worlds that offer many ways to share and communicate, including blogs, videos, interactive games, online ratings, and more.

For each age group below, create a netiquette tip for using interactive technologies (Web 2.0).

Interactive Web sites for children up through age twelve

_____

Interactive Web sites for teenagers

_____

Interactive Web sites for adults

_____

Your Opinion Counts!

As an Internet user, do you think netiquette has anything to do with maintaining FREEDOM on the Internet of the future? Why or why not?

6.3. Cyber Bullying and Netiquette Sense

Learning Objectives

Upon completion of this section you should be able to:

- Discuss how cyber citizenship can lead to a safer online community
- Assess and identify some basic rules in regard to cyber harassment
- Relate the use of netiquette to avoiding cyber harassment
- Identify positive solutions to cyber harassment problems

Cyber Know-How

Bullying has become an online, as well as a physical event. Intimidation online can be just as bad, and in some cases even worse, as bullying that occurs in the physical community.

What Is Cyber Bullying?

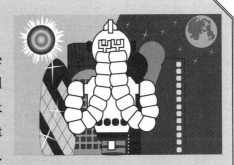

Cyber bullying is a threat that many youth face these days. Unlike the schoolyard bully who relies on physical intimidation, a cyber bully uses words and images to break down a victim. This harassment can occur in e-mail, text messages, instant messages, and chat rooms or on Web sites.

Many youth consider cyber bullying as bad as, or worse than, physical bullying because it can occur 24/7. Unrelenting torment can drive a victim to drastic action.

Terms to Know

Define the following words. Underline and use a dictionary to look up any words you don't know or aren't sure of.

- bully
- cyber harassment
- inadvertent
- threaten

Think About It—Talk About It

How is cyber bullying/harassment a violation of basic cyber citizenship and freedom on the Internet?

Why do some people react in extreme ways to "just words"?

Free Write

Why is it easy to forget basic cyber citizenship guidelines when online? How does this lead to inadvertent cyber harassment of others?

_____

_____

_____

_____

_____

Use Netiquette Sense! It is against the law to threaten someone with physical harm via the Internet. For example, it is against the law to text a message to someone that says: "Watch out, I am going to kill you after school."

Harassment Solutions—Use Netiquette Sense

Your knowledge of netiquette can go a long way in helping to construct solutions to cyber bullying situations.

- As obvious as it may seem, if you are bullied, ignore it or tell a trusted adult. And if you are tempted to bully someone else, don't! Many youth fall into the trap of not thinking about the harmful consequences of unkind messages sent via the Internet because the receiver can't be seen.

- Reread messages to make sure they can't be taken the wrong way. Sometimes things are taken out of context or meant as a joke, but the recipient doesn't realize this and is hurt.
- Use emoticons to help show what you really mean in your messages.

> **Remember:** An online bully is a weak person who resorts to making someone else feel bad to make him- or herself feel better. Stand up to others who bully online, and be a good cyber citizen!

- **Don't be a victim. Get help!** Find an adult who will listen and take you seriously. Unfortunately, this doesn't always happen with the first person you tell. You may have to tell several adults until you find one who will take action. Just remember: Cyber bullying is WRONG—you are RIGHT to get help.
- **Don't open, view, or respond to cyber harassment.** It is beneath you to pay attention to it! Most likely someone is bullying you to make him- or herself feel better.
- **Stay protected.** Never agree to meet with anyone you meet online.
- **Different situations can be resolved in different ways.** An adult can help you find the best solution, whether it be contacting police, having the school take action, etc.

> **Remember:** Getting help is a sign that you are a strong, confident person who will stand up for him- or herself by asking for help! You should never feel ashamed to take steps to make your life, or the life of a friend, better.

Prevention Techniques: How to Keep from Being Bullied Online
- Never share your passwords or PINs with others.
- Remember to log out of any type of networking or communication activities before leaving your computer unattended.
- Think carefully before giving out personal information such as name, address, phone number, school name, or family and friends' names. This information can be used by bullies and others to harm you on the Internet.
- Avoid posting personal photos in public online areas.
- Avoid exchanging pictures or giving out e-mail addresses to people you meet on the Internet.
- Don't send a message when you're angry—it's hard to undo things that are said in anger.
- Delete messages from people you don't know or those from people who seem angry or mean.
- When something doesn't seem right, it probably isn't. Get out of the site, chat, etc.

Use What U Have Learned:

Dear "Online and Helpless" Letters

"Online and Helpless" is our fictional advice column written about online issues people face. Take a look at these three letters and think about how you would help each person. Write a helpful response for each. Include netiquette knowledge and/or outside sources for help that each should consider. Provide tips on how similar problems might be avoided in the future.

Letter 1

Dear "Online and Helpless,"

I attend a school in California. Recently this Web site came out for students. It lets you gossip and post messages online. I just got an e-mail with a link to the site that asks me to FW it to everyone in my address book. Well, I've noticed horrible things posted on the site. Instead of being a fun thing and a way to communicate, people are using it to lie and harass. The messages being posted are getting worse and worse and really starting to hurt people's feelings. So far I've been lucky and nothing has been said about me. But my best friend really got slammed on the site the other day. I feel awful for her and know that this has got to end.

Californian

Your Response:

_____

_____

_____

Letter 2

Dear "Online and Helpless,"

My name is Mark. I'm fourteen. I'm being harassed and I don't know why. I receive e-mails telling me things like "Fourteen days until you die." The countdown goes down each day. I have no idea why anyone would want to do this to me. I'm scared to go to school or even leave the house. What should I do?

Mark

Your Response:

_____

_____

_____

Letter 3

Dear "Online and Helpless,"

I'm not sure why I'm writing you. I don't really want to tell you my name. I'm one of those kids who are always being bullied in school. I'm really smart but just not so good at making friends. Well, I finally got fed up with it recently. I found out my lead tormentor's screen name and password. Well, I "borrowed" his identity to post some fake stuff on eBay. I also had him bid on things. Then I posted his name and phone number on several sites where I also had him say some pretty bad things. So now others are harassing him the way they once harassed me. I think it serves him right! So how come I'm feeling so guilty?

Anonymous

Your Response:

_____

_____

_____

_____

What do you think? Is it legal to create a Web site designed to harass a teacher or principal if a home computer is used?

Although the laws about cyber bullying are still evolving, the legal "rule of thumb" is that if a student-created Web site significantly disrupts the school environment or atmosphere, even if it was created at home, the student and his or her parents can be legally prosecuted by the school or school district.

Cyber Tales—It's the Law

All across the United States, laws are being passed against cyber bullying and harassment. For each state law example below, express your opinion on how the law will or will not help to curb cyber bullying.

Arkansas: A 2007 law added cyber bullying to school anti-bullying policies and included provisions for school officials to take action against some off-campus activities. The law applies to electronic acts whether or not they originate on school property "if the electronic act is directed specifically at students or school personnel and is maliciously intended for the purpose of disrupting school, and has a high likelihood of succeeding in that purpose."

_____

_____

_____

_____

_____

Idaho: A law passed in 2006 allows school officials to temporarily suspend students for disrupting school by bullying or harassing other students, including by using telephones or computers.

_____

_____

_____

_____

_____

Minnesota: A 2007 bill requires schools to create written policies "prohibiting intimidation and bullying of any student," including the use of the Internet.

_____

_____

_____

_____

_____

Washington: A 2007 bill added electronic harassment to school district harassment prevention policies. It calls on school administrators to develop policies prohibiting bulling "via electronic means" but restricts the scope of the policy to actions that take place "while on school grounds and during the school day."

_____

_____

_____

_____

_____

 **Online Extension**

Part 1: Research laws that address cyber bullying in your state. Write a paragraph in the space below to summarize what you found.

_____

_____

_____

_____

_____

Helpful Links
- http://www.cyberbullyalert.com/blog/2008/10/cyber-bullying-state-laws-and-policies/
- http://www.ncsl.org/default.aspx?tabid=12903

Part 2: Research your school's anti-bullying policy and write a paragraph that explains how (or if) the policy addresses cyber bullying. Examples to include: where can a student or parent read the policy (is it on the school Web site?); who should report bullying; how to report bullying and/or cyber bullying at school, and who to report it to; consequences for bullies; does your school district publish district bullying policies on its Web site? Does the school and district follow the law for your state? **Hint:** Cyber bullying policies are sometimes found in the school's Acceptable Use Policy (AUP).

_____

_____

_____

_____

_____

Part 3: Research federal laws on cyber bullying. Write a paragraph that includes what you found out and your opinion on how well the government is addressing the issue.

_____

_____

_____

_____

_____

6.4. Enrichment Activity—Wrap It Up!

Cyber bullying is a problem that many students face but may not necessarily feel comfortable informing others about or reporting concerns. Become involved at your school and help create a way that students can anonymously report any concerns to administration.

Create a D.R.O.P. Box Dealing Responsibly with Online Problems

A D.R.O.P. Box gives your peers a chance to confidentially ask Internet safety questions and report any online concerns. A successful D.R.O.P. Box requires some forethought and communication with administrative staff at your school.

Planning

1. Decide whether the D.R.O.P. Box will be a class project, a committee or team undertaking, or the responsibility of an individual.

2. Ask an adult teacher or counselor to monitor the D.R.O.P. Box and report back to you. He or she should be the only person with access to the box and sort the messages by topic. Any immediate or unsafe concerns must be handled by this adult monitor.

3. Submit a proposal to administration to have a D.R.O.P. Box at your school. In your proposal address the following:

   - Faculty Liaison—What faculty member will be responsible for checking the box?
   - Frequency—How frequently will the faculty member check the box?
   - Chain of Command—Once the faculty member has checked the box, how will issues be handled, that is, what school official will deal with serious or dangerous issues? How will other issues be passed on to students to deal with? How will answers be relayed to the student or school body?

Setting Up the D.R.O.P. Box

1. Find a ballot box and a lock to use.

2. Find a location for your D.R.O.P. Box. Obtain permission to set it up.

3. Monitor box contents.

4. Relay the non-dangerous and non-confidential messages to mentors to address (or handle yourself). Pass along the more serious safety concerns to the school official identified in the proposal for dealing with these issues.

5. Make sure you don't give people the wrong information. **Research and verify your answers before you respond!** Also, please respect the privacy of others. Questions and answers should be publicized anonymously. Don't use people's real names.

6. Relay information back to the student/school body as identified in the proposal. Suggestions include:

   - Periodic articles in the school newspaper (Dear Abby–type column).
   - Daily/weekly spot on school announcements either via PSA or TV spot.
   - Bulletin board in prominent location for posting of answers.

Let i-SAFE Know

Let i-SAFE know about the success of your project.

Contact **mentors@isafe.org** for additional information and support.

6.S. Unit Review

1. Federal and state laws governing Internet activities include laws against:

    a. Downloading and cyber bullying.

    b. Music piracy and posting pictures of other people.

    c. Sending spam and cyber bullying.

    d. Cyber bullying and posting pictures of other people.

2. Netiquette can best be described as:

    a. Widely accepted laws governing online behavior that have evolved over time.

    b. Widely accepted rules of online behavior that have evolved over time.

    c. Emoticons.

    d. A topic that needs to be addressed with new laws.

3. The use of netiquette positively affects the Internet environment by:

    a. Providing a solution for cyber crime.

    b. Minimizing cyber crime.

    c. Eliminating rude and/or abusive online actions.

    d. Minimizing rude, offensive, or abusive online actions.

4. One who uses netiquette would:

    a. Limit sending spam e-mails to ten or fewer per week.

    b. Think before reacting to a flame e-mail.

    c. Only share the contact information of friends with other friends.

    d. Use emoticons when using offensive text language.

5. Netiquette is especially important when using Web 2.0 technologies because:

    a. Laws have been created to govern these technologies.

    b. All of these technologies are for kids.

    c. These technologies involve the interactions of people online.

    d. It is illegal to use offensive language on online social networks.

6. Good advice for someone who says he or she has received an e-mail that contains a harassing message from a classmate would include:

   a. Reread the message carefully before jumping to conclusions.

   b. Send no more than one e-mail response.

   c. Send an e-mail to all of your friends, asking them to ignore the "bully" at school.

   d. Call the police.

7. It is always against the law to:

   a. Send a flame e-mail.

   b. Threaten another with physical harm via e-mail.

   c. Neither a nor b.

   d Both a and b.

8. Cyber bullying prevention techniques include:

   a. Remembering to log out of programs before leaving your computer unattended.

   b. Avoiding sending messages when you are angry or upset.

   c. Avoiding posting personal photos in public online areas.

   d. All of the above.

9. Which one of the following statements is TRUE?

   a. Because of free speech, one cannot get in trouble for cyber bullying if the computer used is in one's home.

   b. Cyber bullying includes harassment through the use of computers, but not through the use of cell phones.

   c. Cyber bullying includes harassment through the use of computers and cell phones.

   d. Cyber bullying becomes a crime only if the victim is eventually hurt physically.

10. Providing a way for students to confidentially ask Internet safety questions and report any online concerns is an important step in helping to create a safer online environment because:

   a. Most teachers don't consider it to be a problem.

   b. Cyber bullying victims may feel afraid or be too embarrassed to tell others about their problem.

   c. There are no laws to protect victims of cyber harassment.

   d. Bullying is a problem that should not be talked about.

INDEX

A

Acceptable use policy (AUP), v; tip, 3, 8–9, 10, 29, 33, 65, 68, 186, 206

Acronyms: defined, 98, 183, 196; used in IM (instant messaging), 98

Anonymity online, 33, 149

Anonymous, defined, 92

Anti-bullying policy, researching, 206

Appropriate, defined, 92

Arkansas, school anti-bullying policy, 204–205

Attachments, 34, 54–55, 69, 97; and computer viruses, 34

B

Barriers, breaking down, 161–162

Beyond Revealing Simple Information activity, 97, 119–121; digital technology and sharing of information, 119–120; Global Positioning System (GPS), 121; learning objectives, 119; Sharing Picture Activity answer key, 119; terms to know, 119; Use What U Have Learned, 120; Use What U Have Learned answer key, 119

Blogs, 97, 112; and bullying, 81, 83

Buddy Lists, 170

Building trust, 162

Bullying, *See* Cyber bullying

C

Cell phone, global positioning system (GPS), 121

Cellphone pictures, 97

Chat sites, and bullying, 81, 83

Circle of Friends activity, 17

Citizen, defined, 41

Common-Sense Approach to Strangers Online unit (grades 5–8), vii, *See* Online strangers unit (grades 5–8)

Community Crossword, 35, 56

Community, defined, 7, 41

Computer programs, 53

Computer viruses, 53; and attachments, 34

Consequences, 71, 73–75

Cyber bullying, 199–208, *See also* Cyber bullying unit (grades 3–4); anti-bullying policy, researching, 206; and chat sites, 81, 83; defined, 81, 199; laws against, 204–205; prevention techniques, 201

Cyber Bullying and Netiquette Sense activity, 185, 199–206; Cyber Know-How, 199; Cyber Tales, 185, 204–205; definitions, 185; Free Write, 200; harassment solutions, 200–201; helpful links, 206; learning objectives, 199; Online and Helpless Activity, 185, 203–204; online

extension, 184–186, 206; questions, 185; terms to know, 198–200

Cyber bullying unit (grades 3–4), vi, 63–86; activities, 68–72; additional resources, 65; consequences, 73–75; Cyberspace as a Global Community activity, 70–71, 81–83; Enrichment Activity—Wrap It Up!, 207–208; format plan, 66; group empowerment activity ideas, 71; group-guided implementation, 66; happy slapping, 70; Heroes Against Cyber Bullying activity, 68, 73; Heroes Can Be Everyday People Too! activity, 77; implementation options, 66–67; Kind vs. Unkind activity, 70, 81; lesson preparation, 65–66; Now Think About an Online Hero activity, 78; post-assessment reminder, 71; semi-self-guided implementation, 67; small-group implementation, 66–67; Sticks and Stones activity, 68, 80; student pages, 73–86; survey, creating, 68, 75; teacher's guide, 65–67; Tips To End Cyber Bullying activity, 71, 84–85; unit format, 65; unit goal, 65; unit review, 209–210; vocabulary check, 73, 78–79; What Is a Hero? activity, 69, 77; Write a Cyber Tale activity, 70–72, 86

Cyber citizenship and netiquette sense unit (grades 5–8), vi, 178–210, *See also* Cyber bullying; Netiquette; activities, 182–186; additional resources, 179; citizenship know-how, 190; Cyber Bullying and Netiquette Sense activity, 185–186, 199–206; Enrichment Activity—Wrap It Up, 186, 207; format plan, 180; Free Write, 191; Go Online, 192; Go Online answer key, 182; group-guided implementation, 180; implementation options, 180–181; Judge and Jury answer key, 184; lesson/activity sections, 179; lesson preparation, 179–180; netiquette, defined, 193; Put it Together answer key, 182; Rules, Laws, and Ethics activity, 189–191; semi-self-guided implementation, 181; small-group implementation, 181; student pages, 187–188; teacher's guide, 178–181; Terms to Know answer key, 183; Texting Know-How answer key, 183; Think About It—Talk About It answer key, 182; tip, creating, 184; Understanding Netiquette activity, 183–184, 193–198; unit format, 179; unit goal, 179; unit review, 186

Cyber community, 7

Cyber Tales, 107, 112, 125–126, 166–167, 185, 204–205

Cyberethics, *See* Ethics

Cyberspace, 37–38; defined, 37; getting lost in, 46–47; as a global community, 70–71, 81–83

D

Digital footprints, 95, 113–114

Digital technology, and sharing of information, 119–120

Diving into Internet safety (grades K–1), *See* Internet safety unit

D.R.O.P. box, 186, 207–208